Fred & Marjorie

For Jordy, Jonah, and Dahlia — D.K.

To my mom. And to my aunt's golden retrievers — they helped me overcome my fear of dogs, and now I can't imagine life without them — A.P.

Fred & Marjorie

A DOCTOR, A DOG, AND THE DISCOVERY OF INSULIN

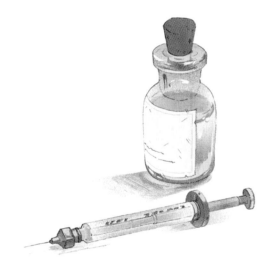

Deborah Kerbel

Illustrated by Angela Poon

Owlkids Books

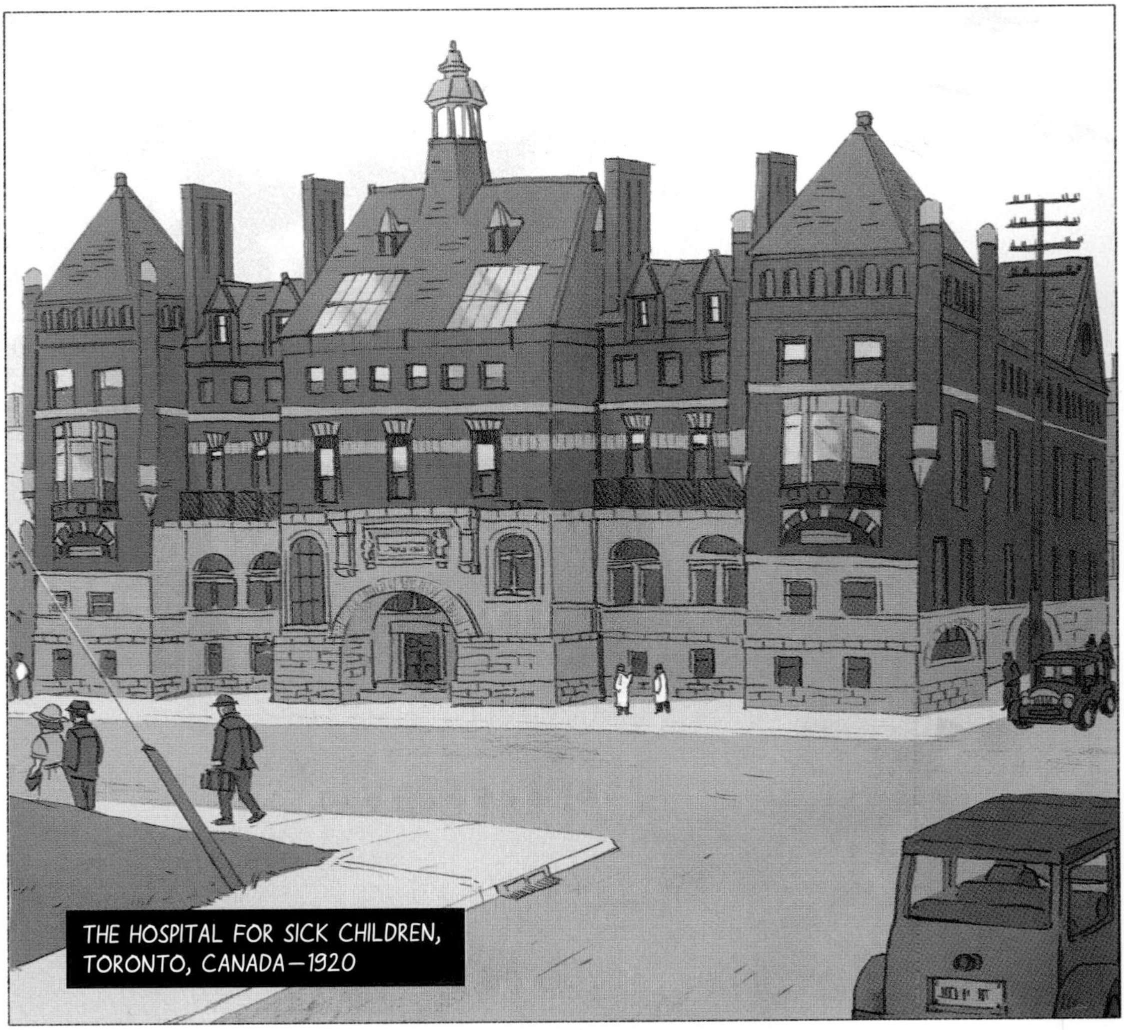
THE HOSPITAL FOR SICK CHILDREN,
TORONTO, CANADA—1920

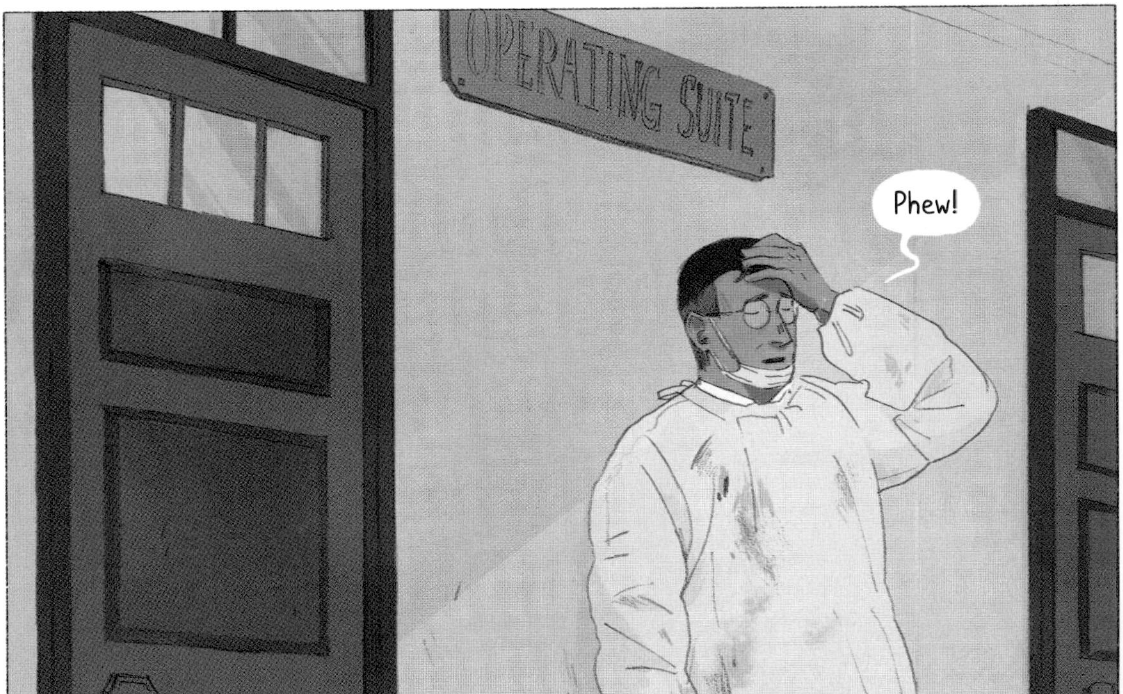
OPERATING SUITE
Phew!

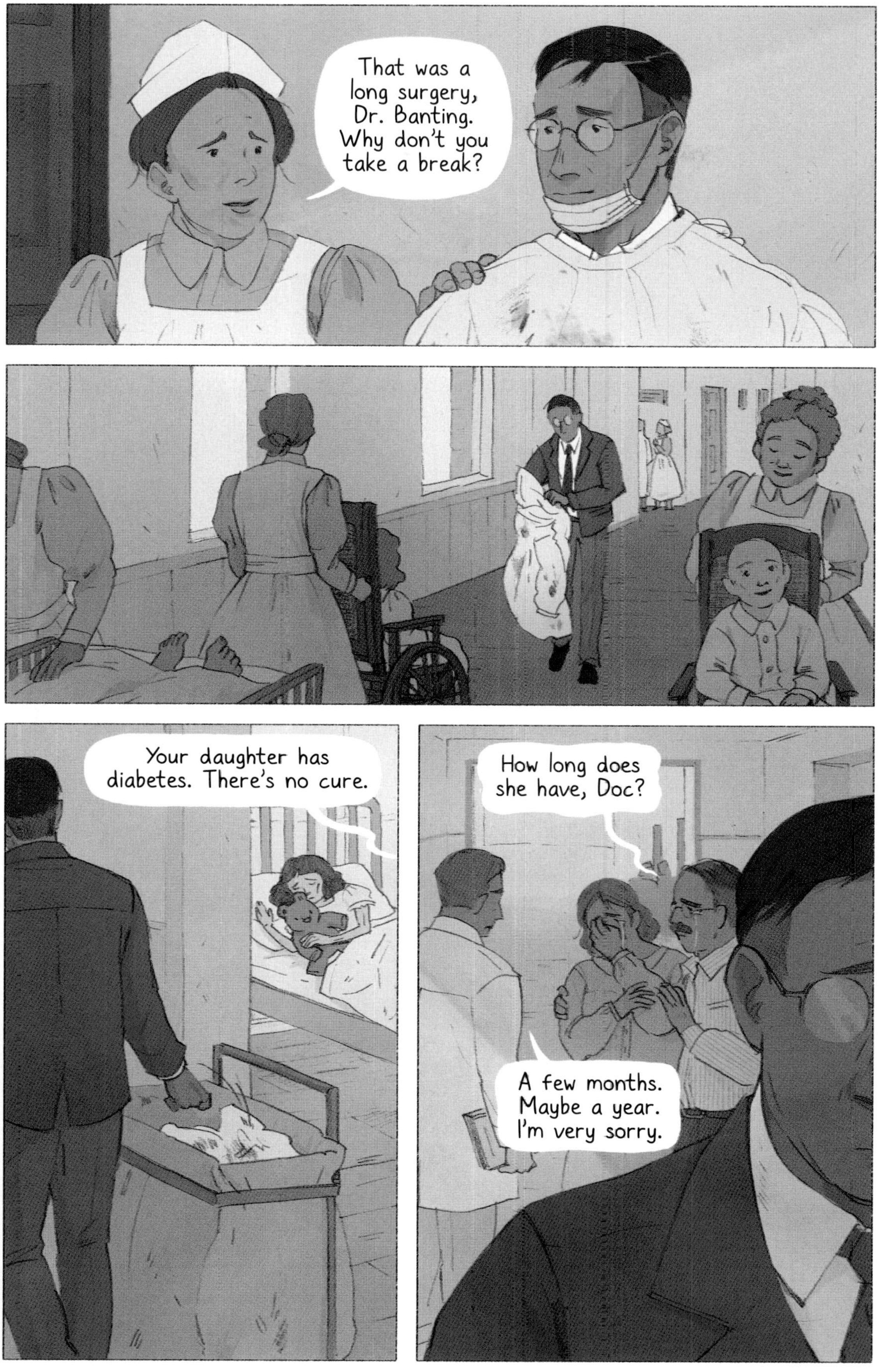
That was a long surgery, Dr. Banting. Why don't you take a break?
Your daughter has diabetes. There's no cure.
How long does she have, Doc?
A few months. Maybe a year. I'm very sorry.

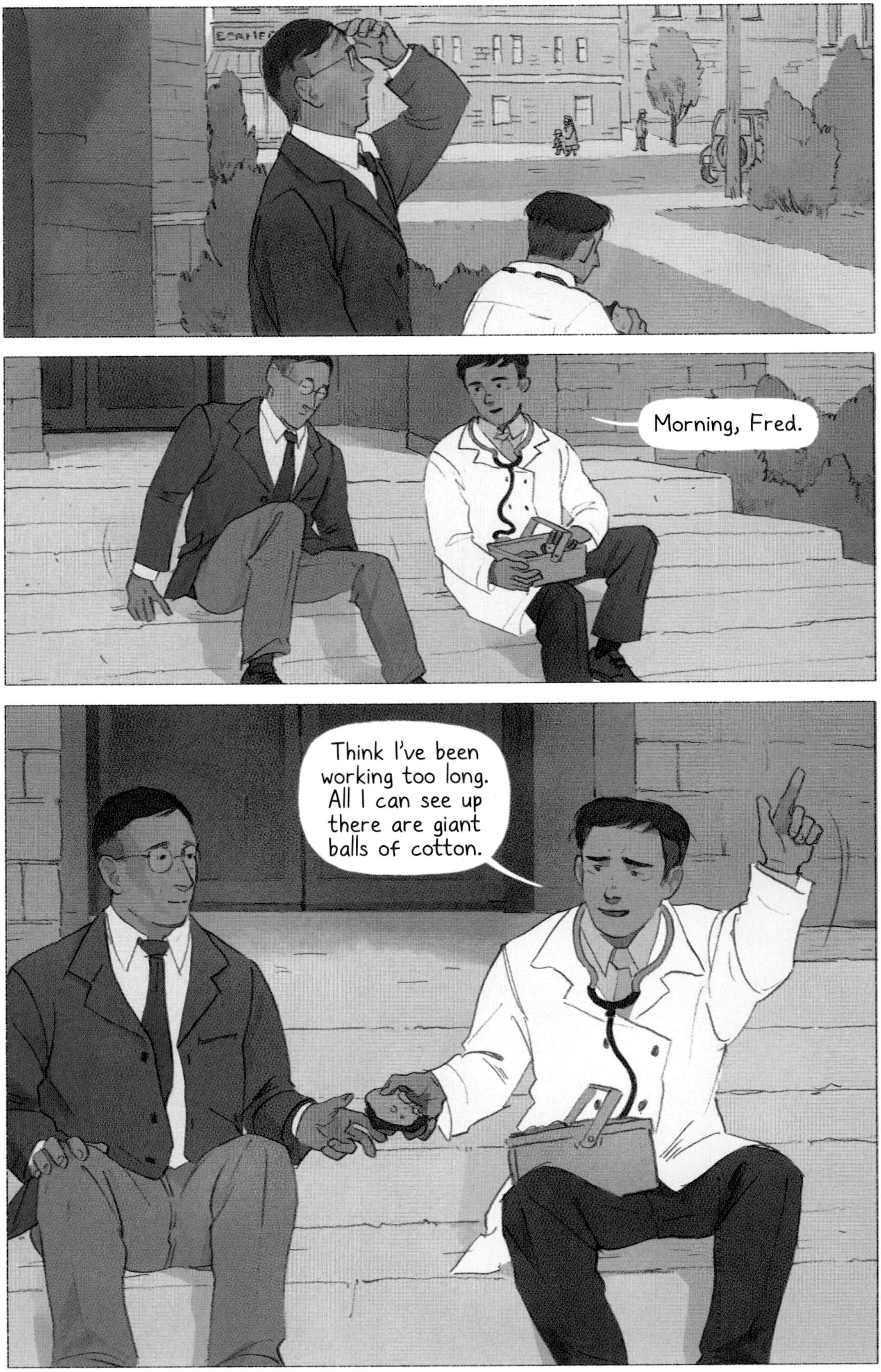
Morning, Fred.
Think I've been working too long. All I can see up there are giant balls of cotton.

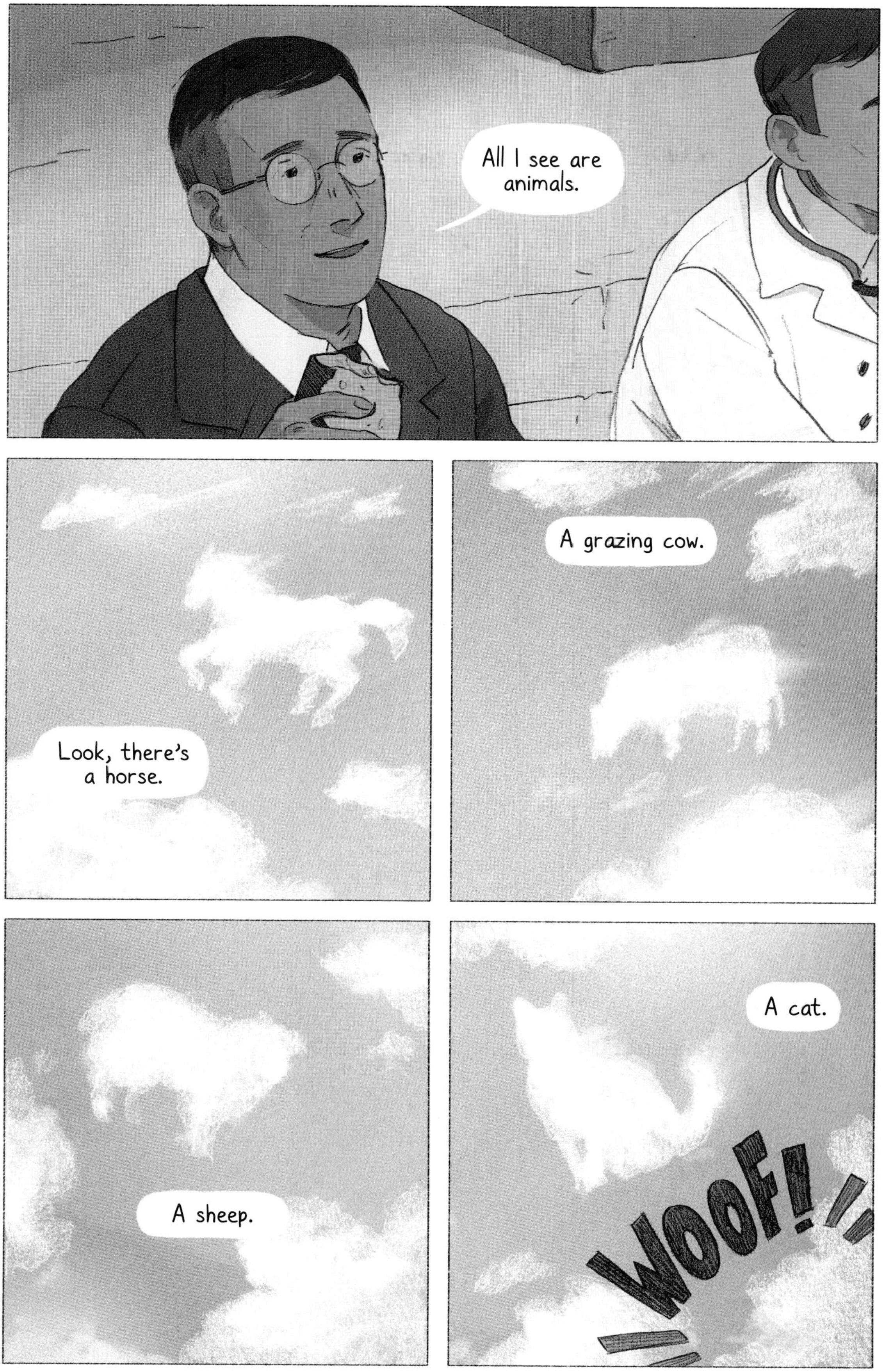
All I see are animals.
Look, there's a horse.
A grazing cow.
A sheep.
A cat.
WOOF!

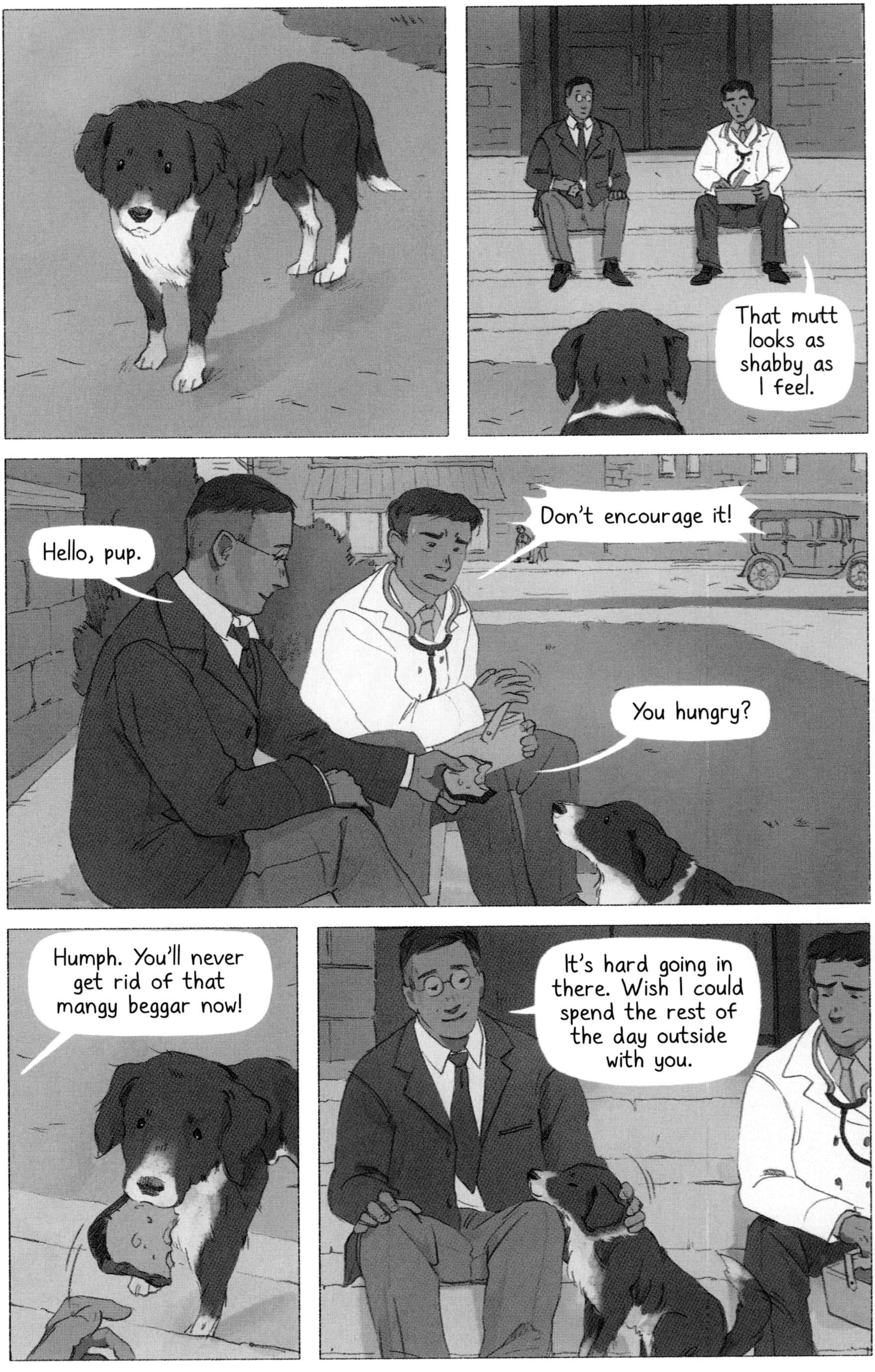

That mutt looks as shabby as I feel.
Hello, pup.
Don't encourage it!
You hungry?
Humph. You'll never get rid of that mangy beggar now!
It's hard going in there. Wish I could spend the rest of the day outside with you.

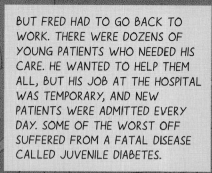

BUT FRED HAD TO GO BACK TO WORK. THERE WERE DOZENS OF YOUNG PATIENTS WHO NEEDED HIS CARE. HE WANTED TO HELP THEM ALL, BUT HIS JOB AT THE HOSPITAL WAS TEMPORARY, AND NEW PATIENTS WERE ADMITTED EVERY DAY. SOME OF THE WORST OFF SUFFERED FROM A FATAL DISEASE CALLED JUVENILE DIABETES.

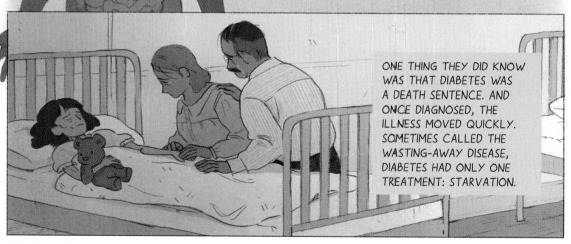

IN 1920, DOCTORS KNEW THAT DIABETES PREVENTED A BODY FROM BREAKING DOWN SUGAR. THEY'D ALSO DISCOVERED THAT THE DISEASE HAD SOMETHING TO DO WITH A PART OF THE DIGESTIVE SYSTEM CALLED THE PANCREAS. BUT THEY DIDN'T YET UNDERSTAND HOW.

ONE THING THEY DID KNOW WAS THAT DIABETES WAS A DEATH SENTENCE. AND ONCE DIAGNOSED, THE ILLNESS MOVED QUICKLY. SOMETIMES CALLED THE WASTING-AWAY DISEASE, DIABETES HAD ONLY ONE TREATMENT: STARVATION.

THERE HAD TO BE A BETTER WAY TO HELP KIDS WITH DIABETES.

BUT NO DOCTOR HAD BEEN ABLE TO FIND THE ANSWER.

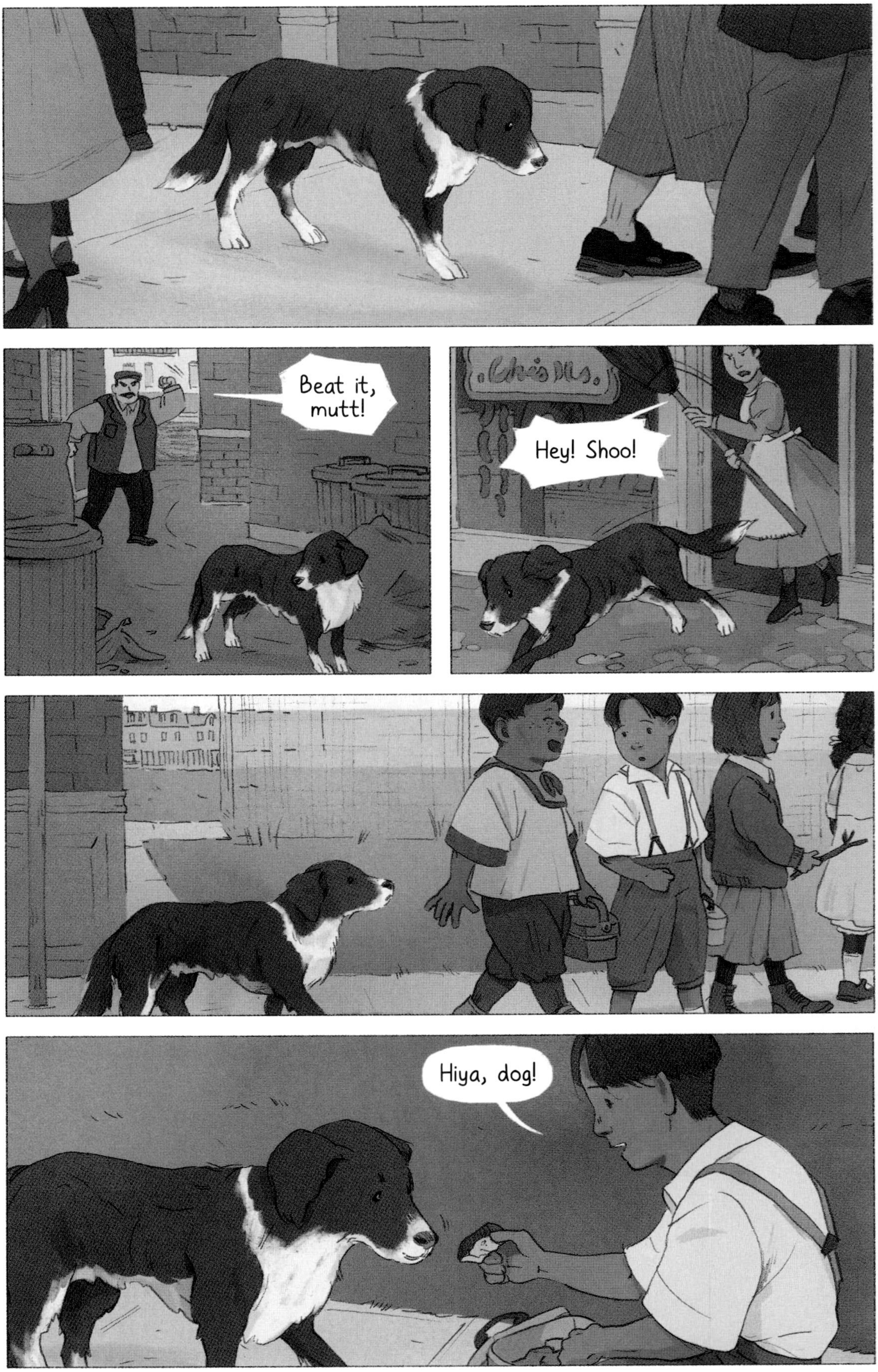
Beat it, mutt!
Hey! Shoo!
Hiya, dog!

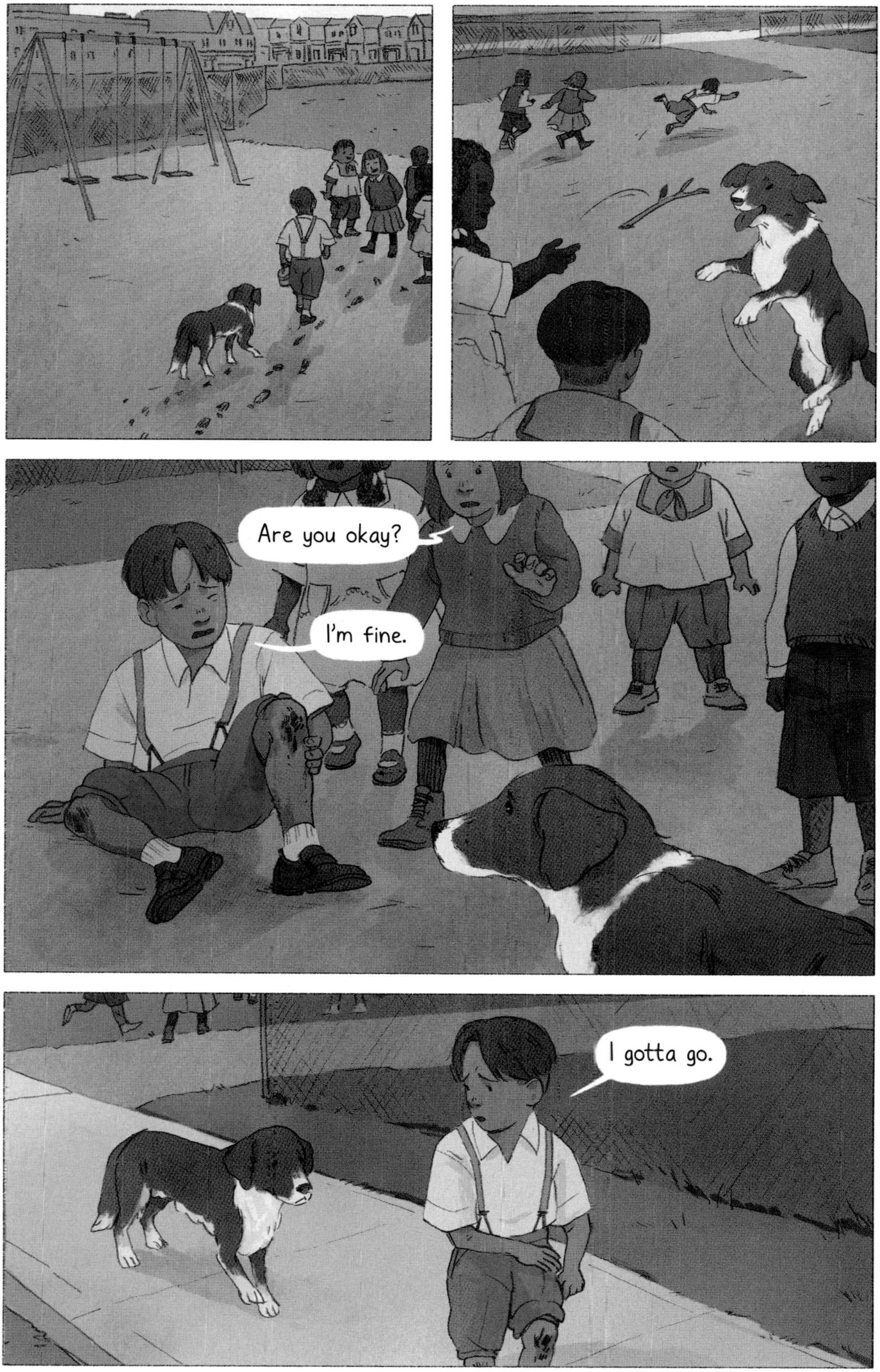
Are you okay?
I'm fine.
I gotta go.

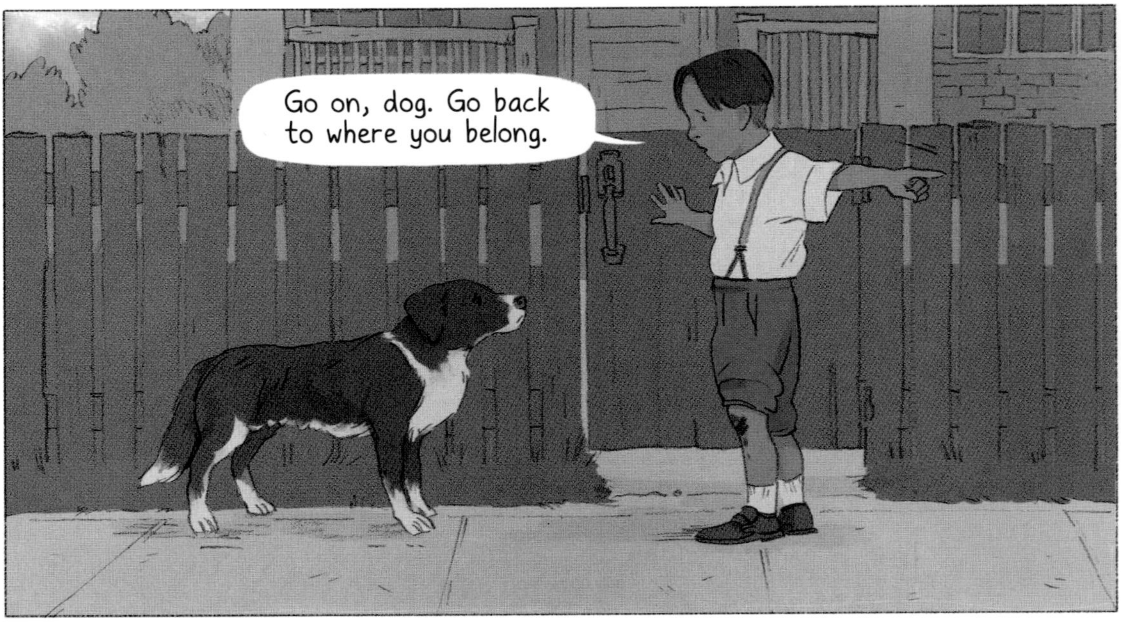
Go on, dog. Go back to where you belong.

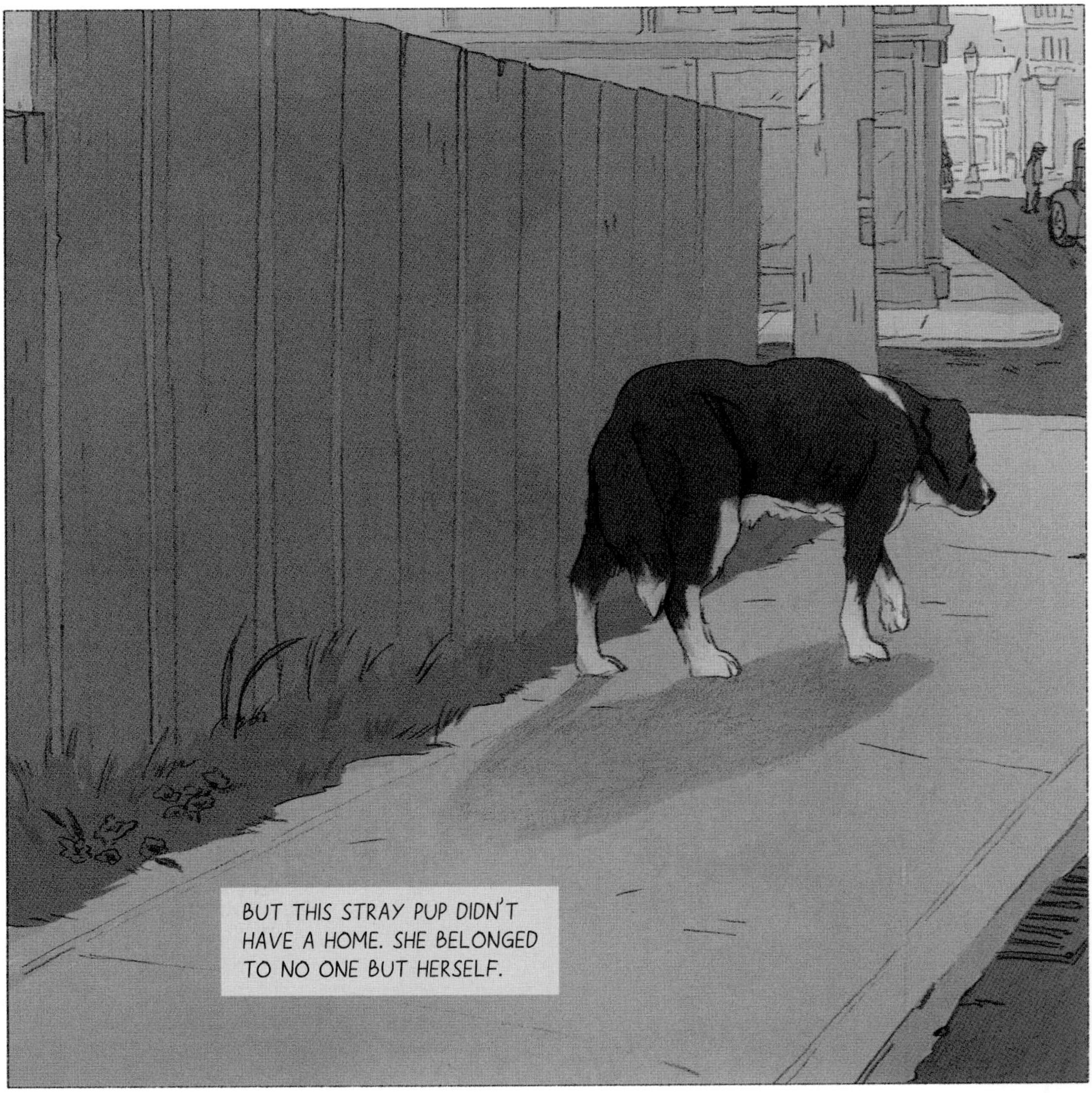
BUT THIS STRAY PUP DIDN'T HAVE A HOME. SHE BELONGED TO NO ONE BUT HERSELF.

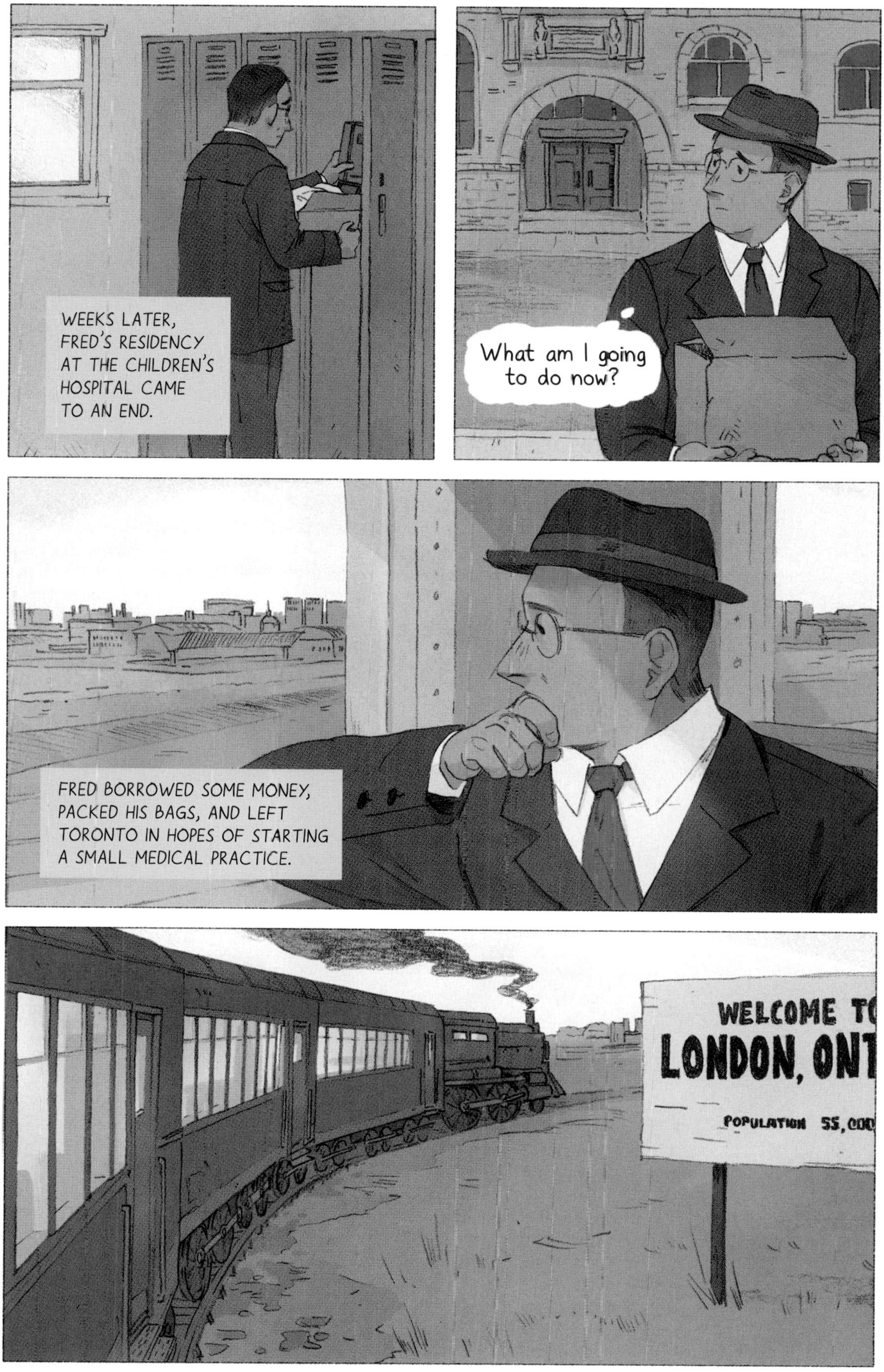
WEEKS LATER, FRED'S RESIDENCY AT THE CHILDREN'S HOSPITAL CAME TO AN END.
What am I going to do now?
FRED BORROWED SOME MONEY, PACKED HIS BAGS, AND LEFT TORONTO IN HOPES OF STARTING A SMALL MEDICAL PRACTICE.
WELCOME TO
LONDON, ONT
POPULATION 55,00

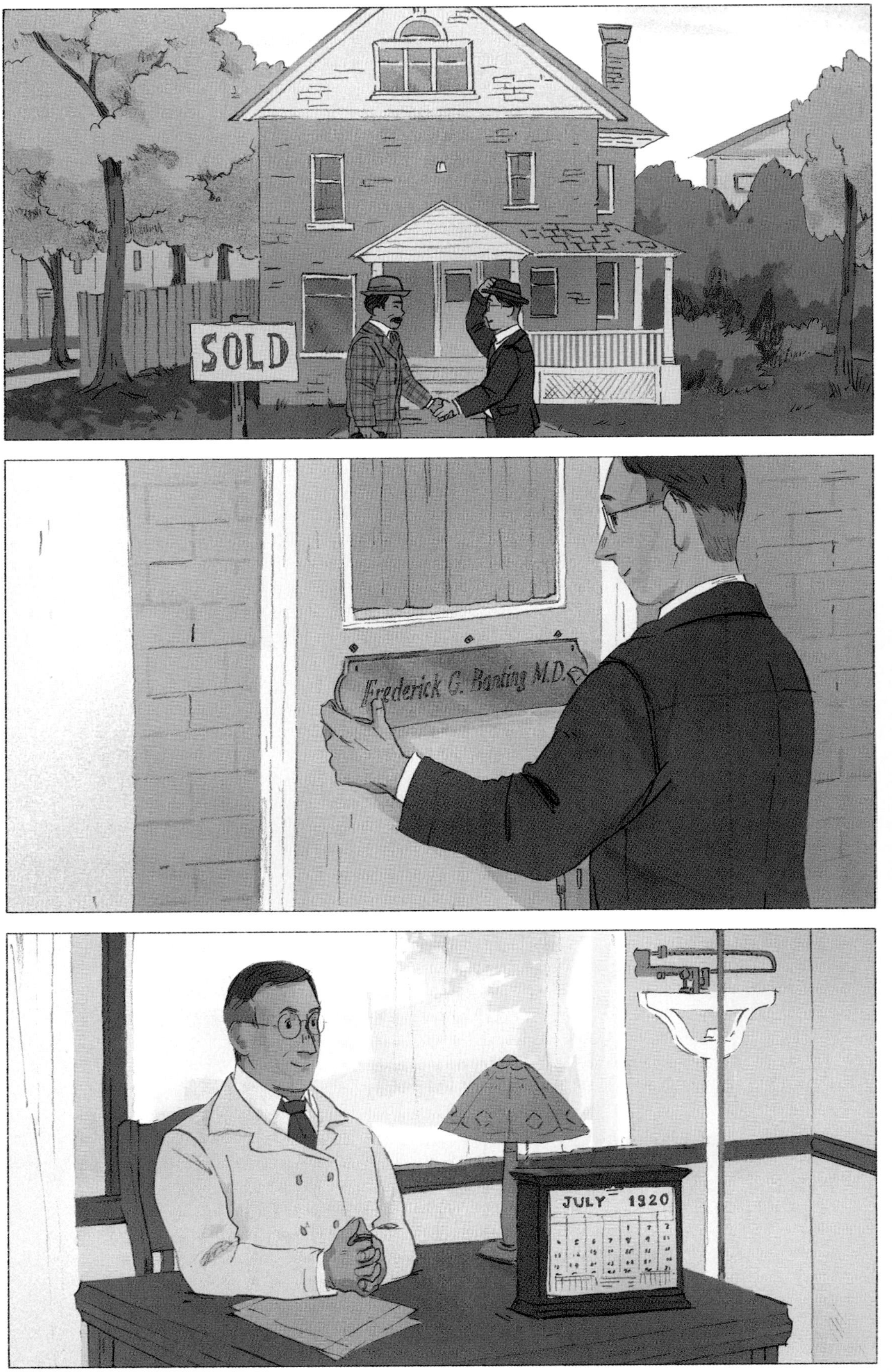
SOLD
Frederick G. Banting M.D.
JULY 1920

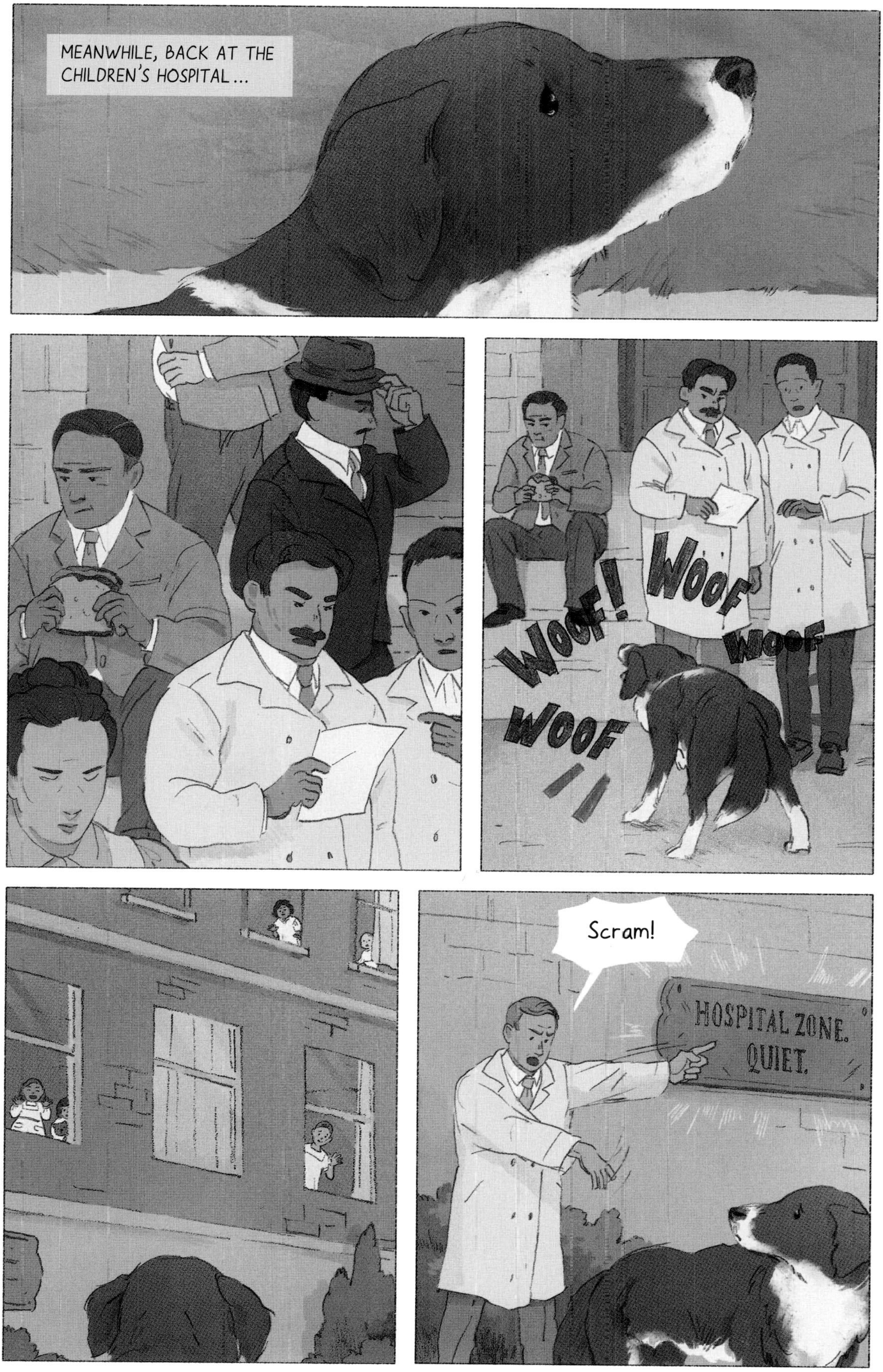
MEANWHILE, BACK AT THE CHILDREN'S HOSPITAL...
WOOF!
WOOF
WOOF
WOOF
WOOF
Scram!
HOSPITAL ZONE. QUIET.

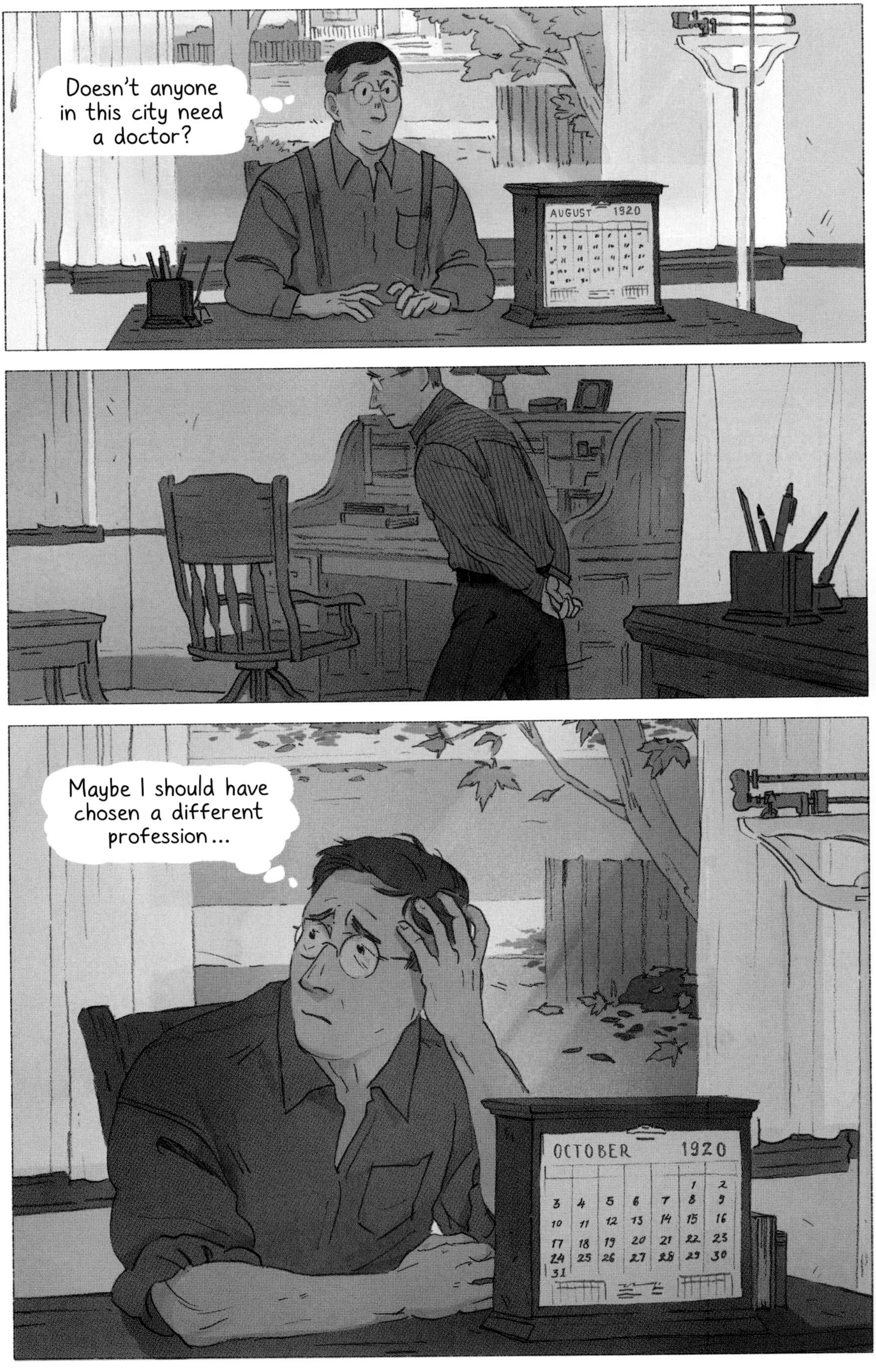
Doesn't anyone in this city need a doctor?
AUGUST 1920
Maybe I should have chosen a different profession...
OCTOBER 1920

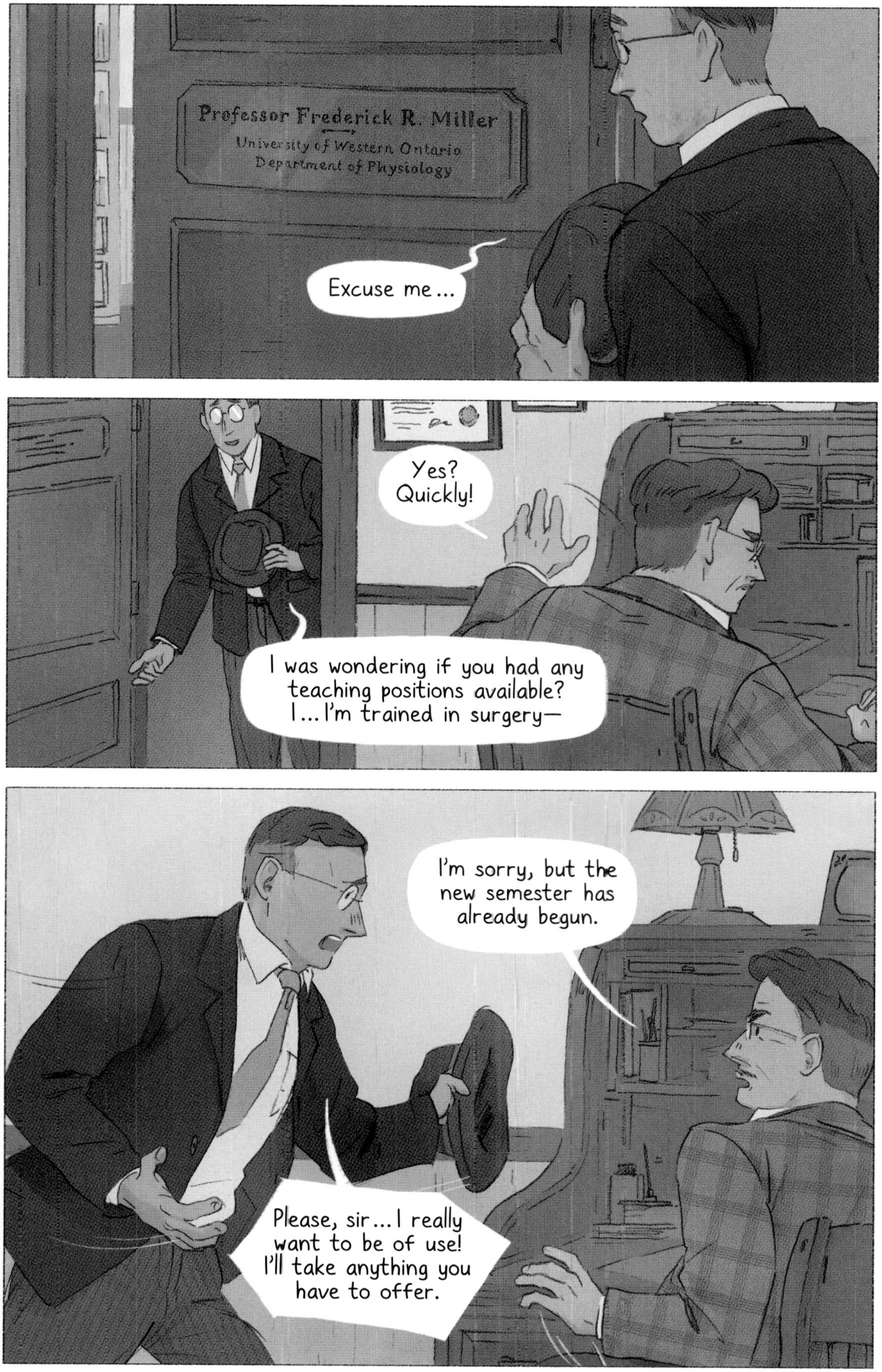
Professor Frederick R. Miller
University of Western Ontario
Department of Physiology
Excuse me...
Yes? Quickly!
I was wondering if you had any teaching positions available? I... I'm trained in surgery—
I'm sorry, but the new semester has already begun.
Please, sir... I really want to be of use! I'll take anything you have to offer.

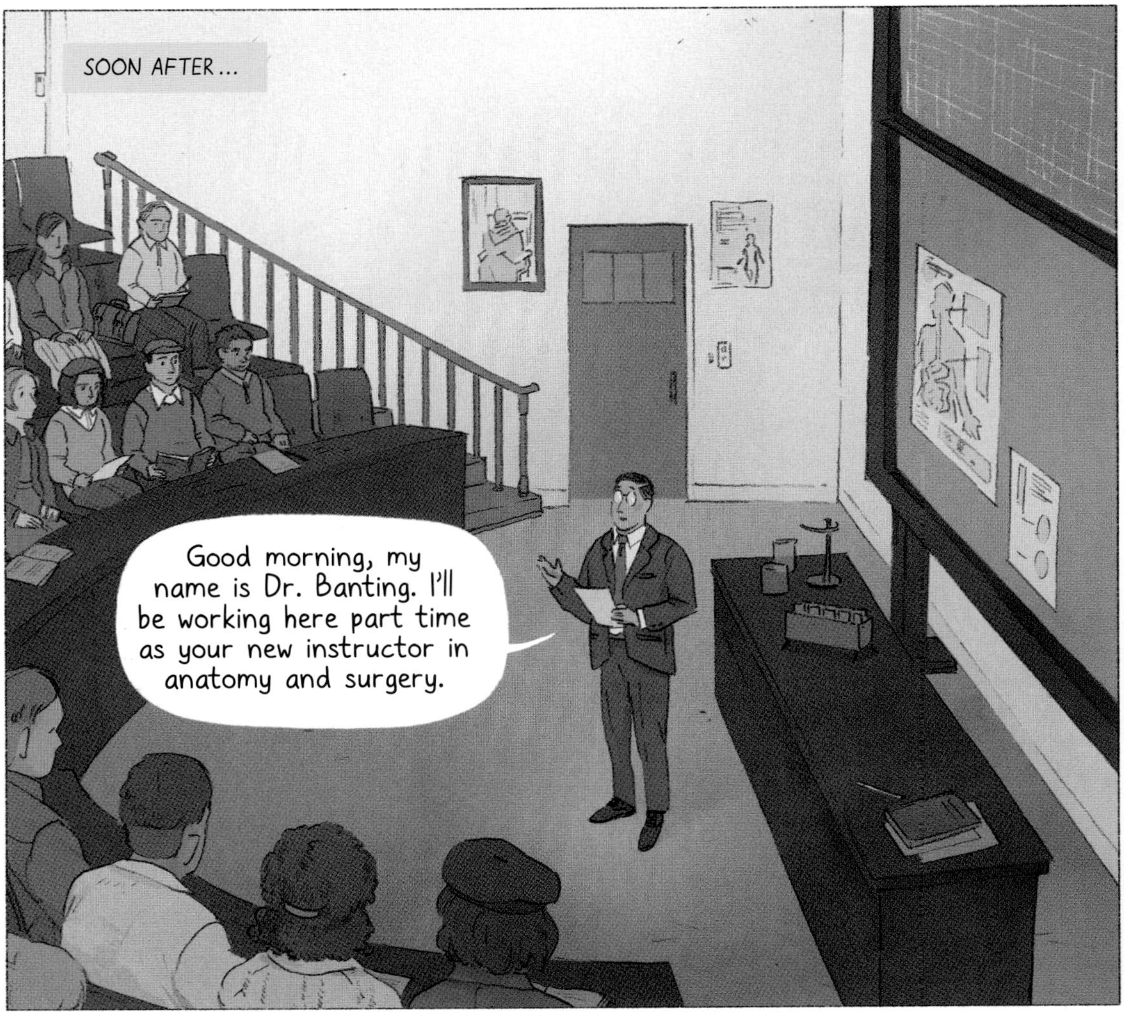
SOON AFTER...
Good morning, my name is Dr. Banting. I'll be working here part time as your new instructor in anatomy and surgery.

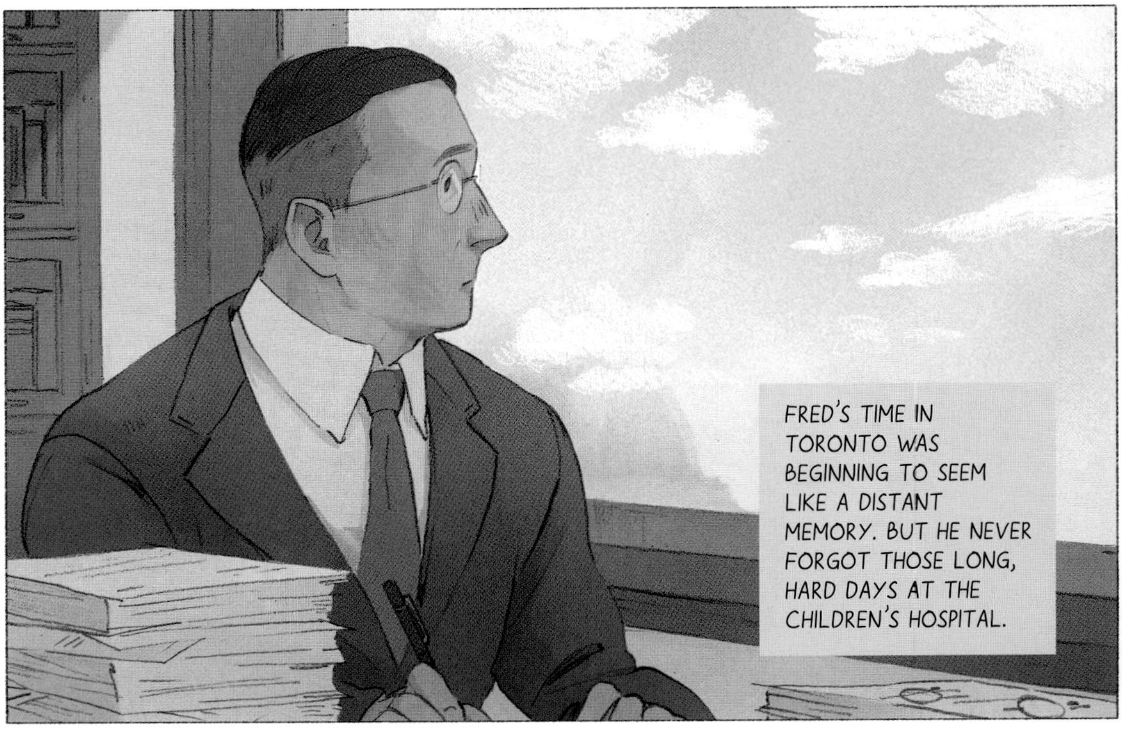
FRED'S TIME IN TORONTO WAS BEGINNING TO SEEM LIKE A DISTANT MEMORY. BUT HE NEVER FORGOT THOSE LONG, HARD DAYS AT THE CHILDREN'S HOSPITAL.

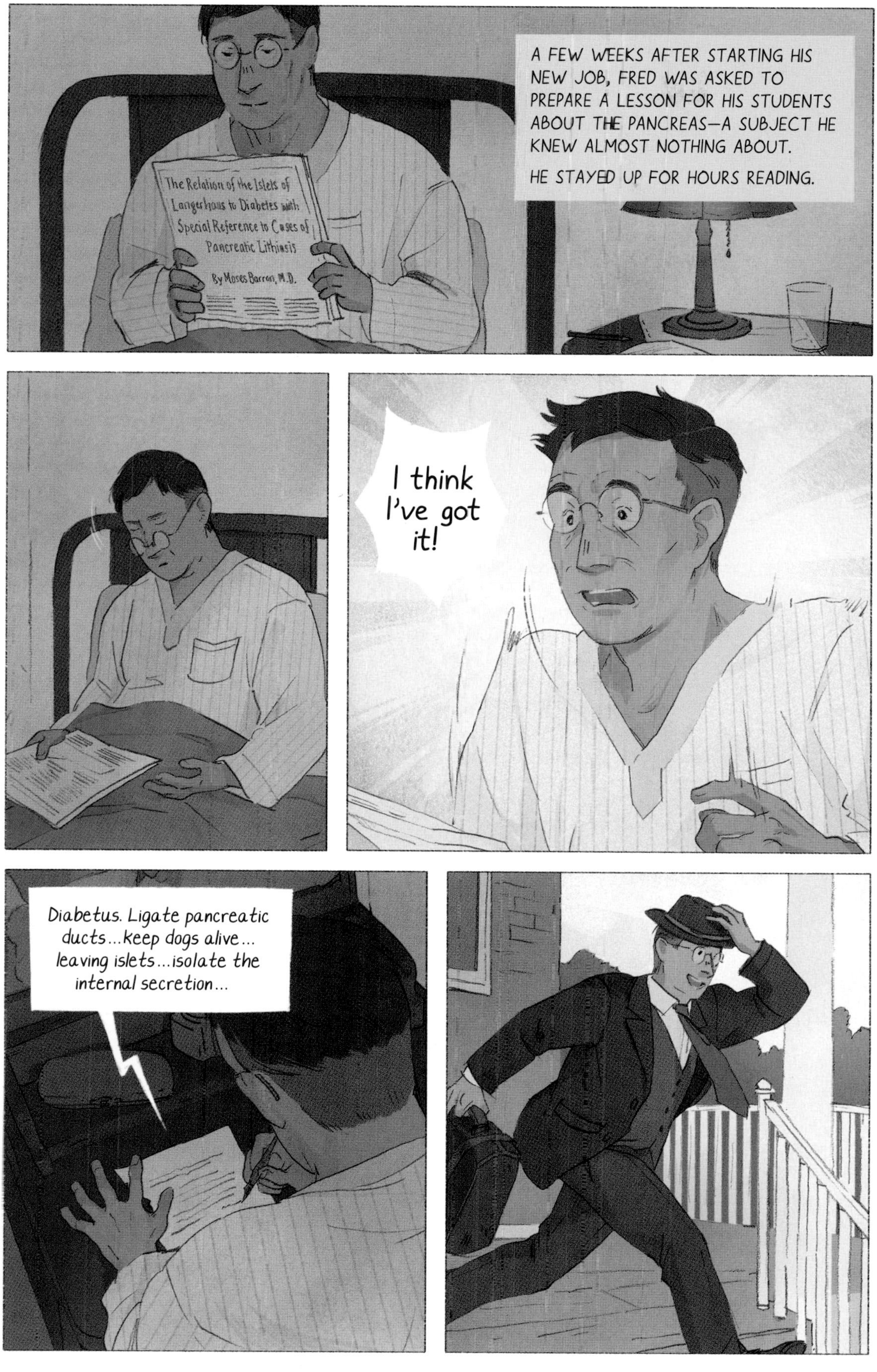
A FEW WEEKS AFTER STARTING HIS NEW JOB, FRED WAS ASKED TO PREPARE A LESSON FOR HIS STUDENTS ABOUT THE PANCREAS—A SUBJECT HE KNEW ALMOST NOTHING ABOUT.
HE STAYED UP FOR HOURS READING.
The Relation of the Islets of Langerhans to Diabetes with Special Reference to Cases of Pancreatic Lithiasis
By Moses Barron, M.D.
I think I've got it!
Diabetus. Ligate pancreatic ducts...keep dogs alive... leaving islets...isolate the internal secretion...

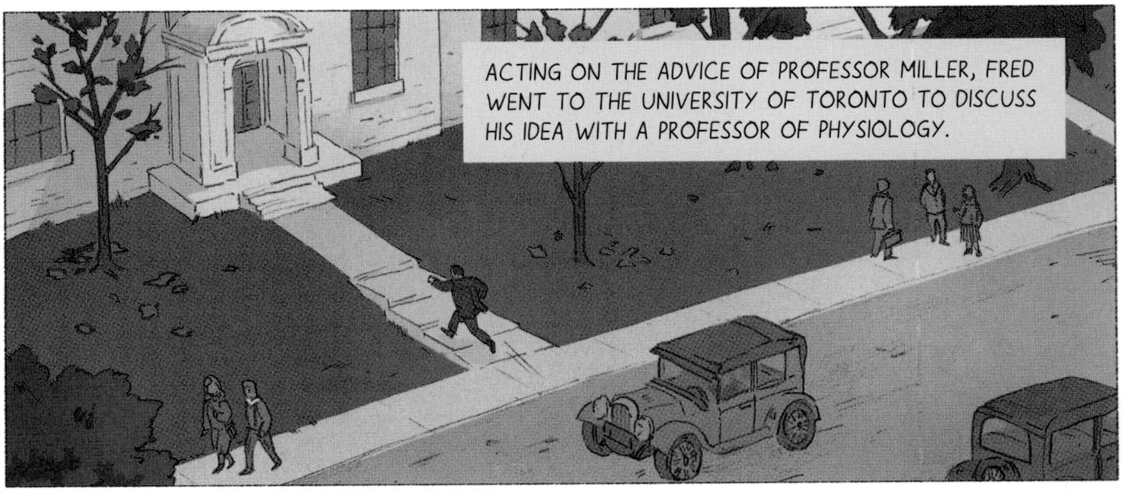
ACTING ON THE ADVICE OF PROFESSOR MILLER, FRED WENT TO THE UNIVERSITY OF TORONTO TO DISCUSS HIS IDEA WITH A PROFESSOR OF PHYSIOLOGY.

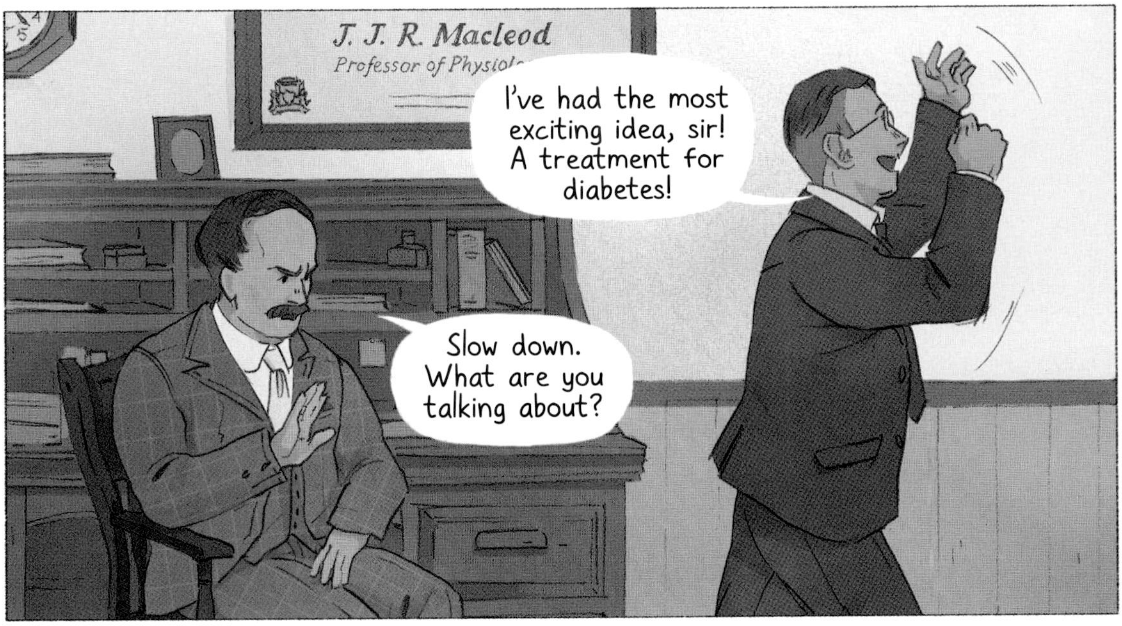
J. J. R. Macleod
I've had the most exciting idea, sir! A treatment for diabetes!
Slow down. What are you talking about?

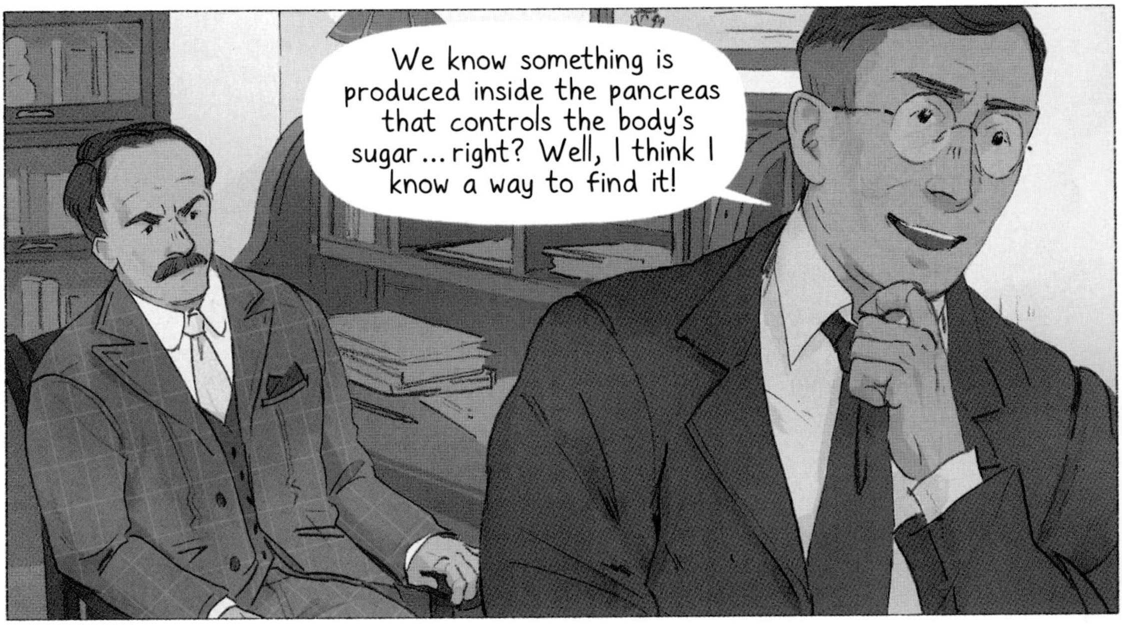
We know something is produced inside the pancreas that controls the body's sugar... right? Well, I think I know a way to find it!

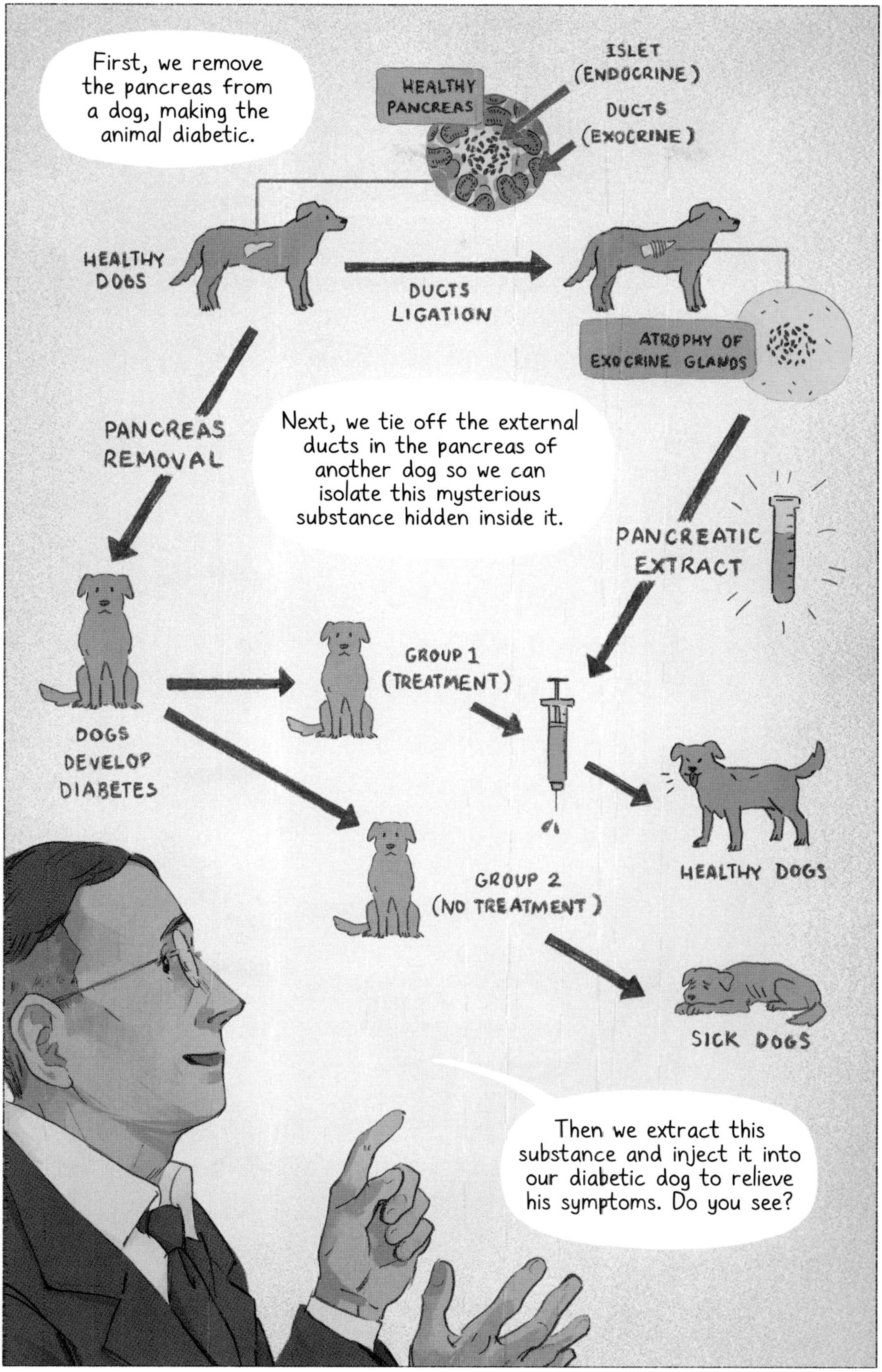
First, we remove the pancreas from a dog, making the animal diabetic.
HEALTHY PANCREAS
ISLET (ENDOCRINE)
DUCTS (EXOCRINE)
HEALTHY DOGS
DUCTS LIGATION
ATROPHY OF EXOCRINE GLANDS
PANCREAS REMOVAL
Next, we tie off the external ducts in the pancreas of another dog so we can isolate this mysterious substance hidden inside it.
PANCREATIC EXTRACT
GROUP 1 (TREATMENT)
DOGS DEVELOP DIABETES
HEALTHY DOGS
GROUP 2 (NO TREATMENT)
SICK DOGS
Then we extract this substance and inject it into our diabetic dog to relieve his symptoms. Do you see?

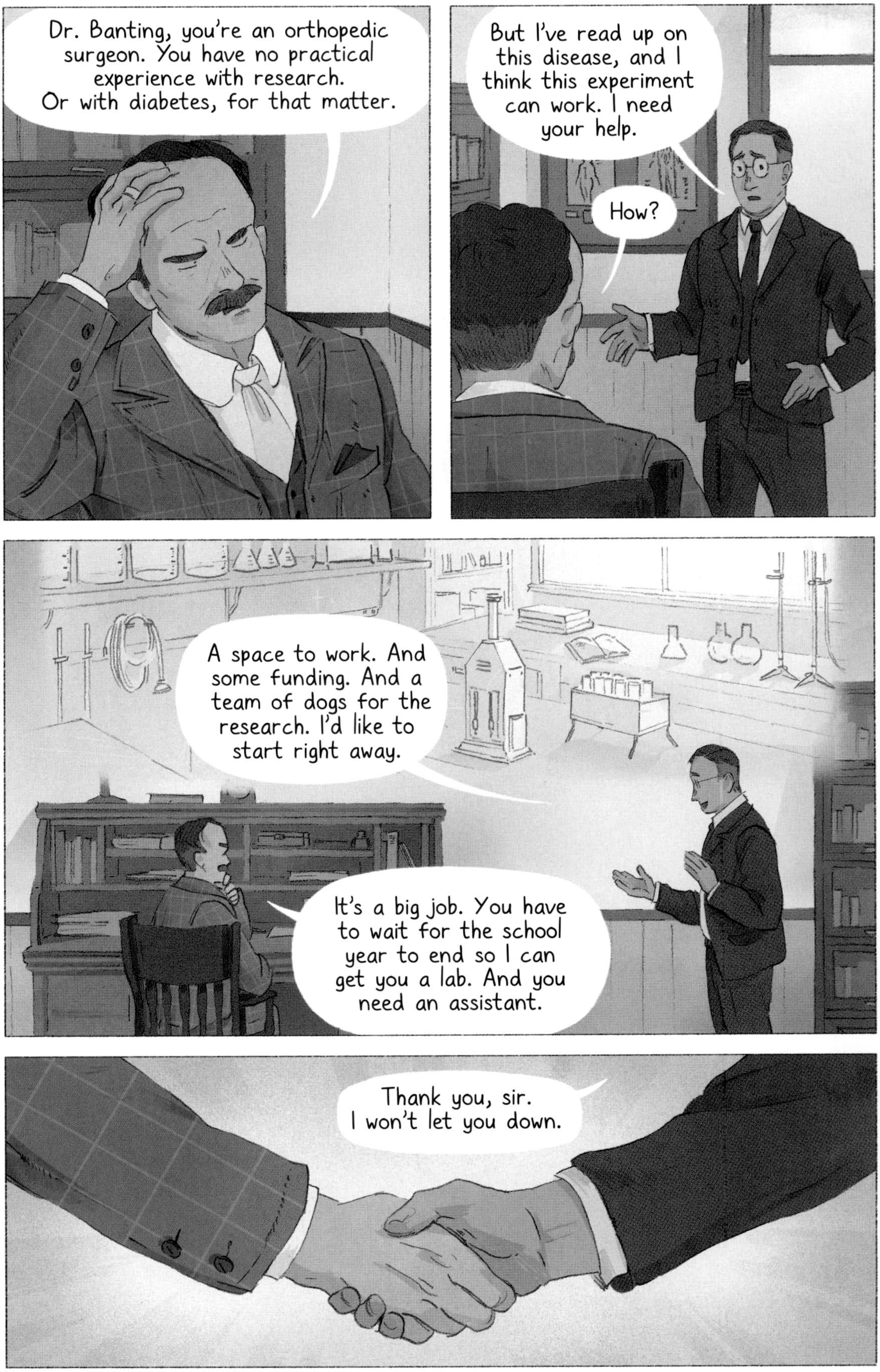
Dr. Banting, you're an orthopedic surgeon. You have no practical experience with research. Or with diabetes, for that matter.
But I've read up on this disease, and I think this experiment can work. I need your help.
How?
A space to work. And some funding. And a team of dogs for the research. I'd like to start right away.
It's a big job. You have to wait for the school year to end so I can get you a lab. And you need an assistant.
Thank you, sir. I won't let you down.

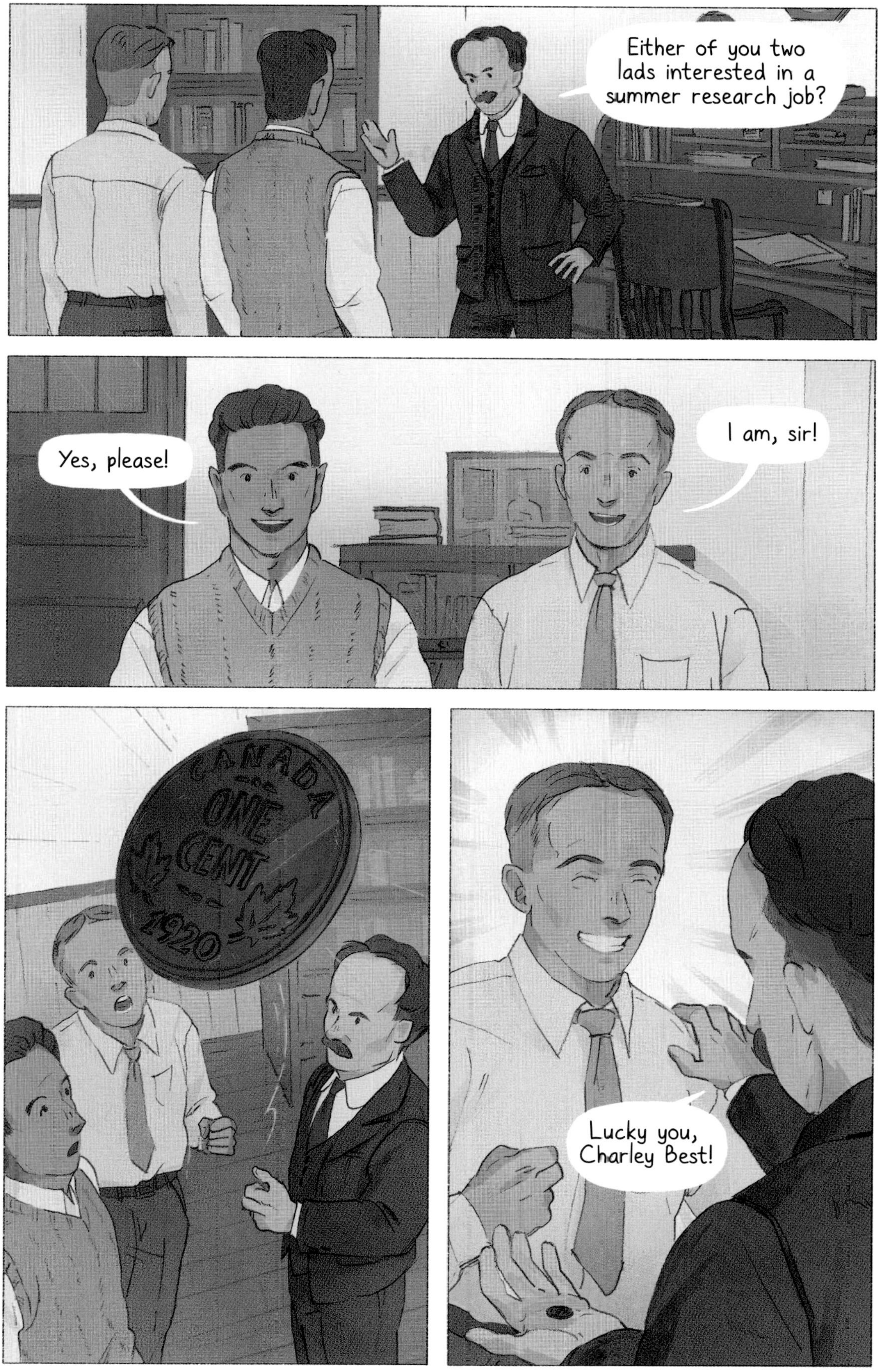
Either of you two lads interested in a summer research job?
Yes, please!
I am, sir!
CANADA
ONE CENT
1920
Lucky you, Charley Best!

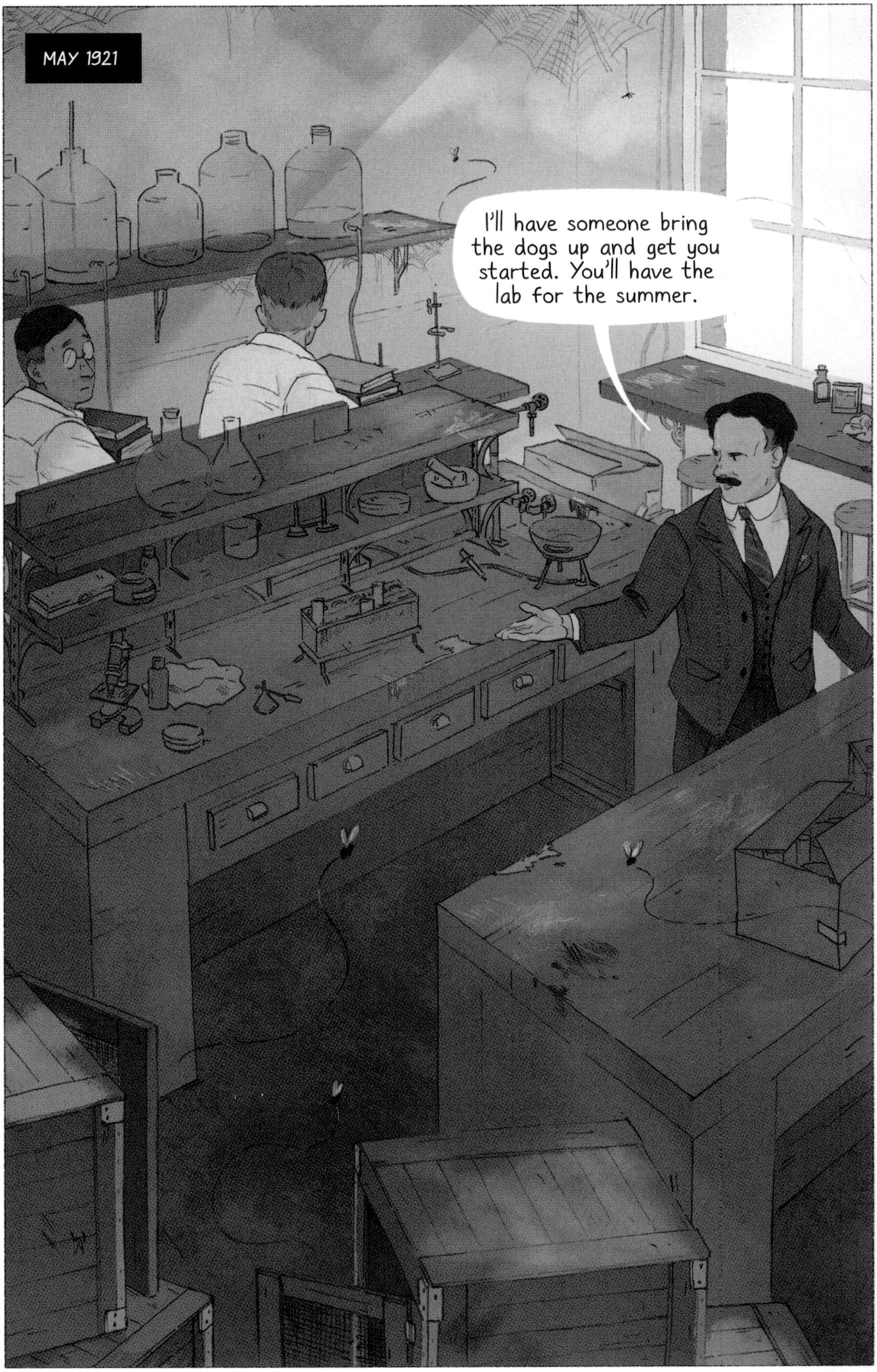
MAY 1921
I'll have someone bring the dogs up and get you started. You'll have the lab for the summer.

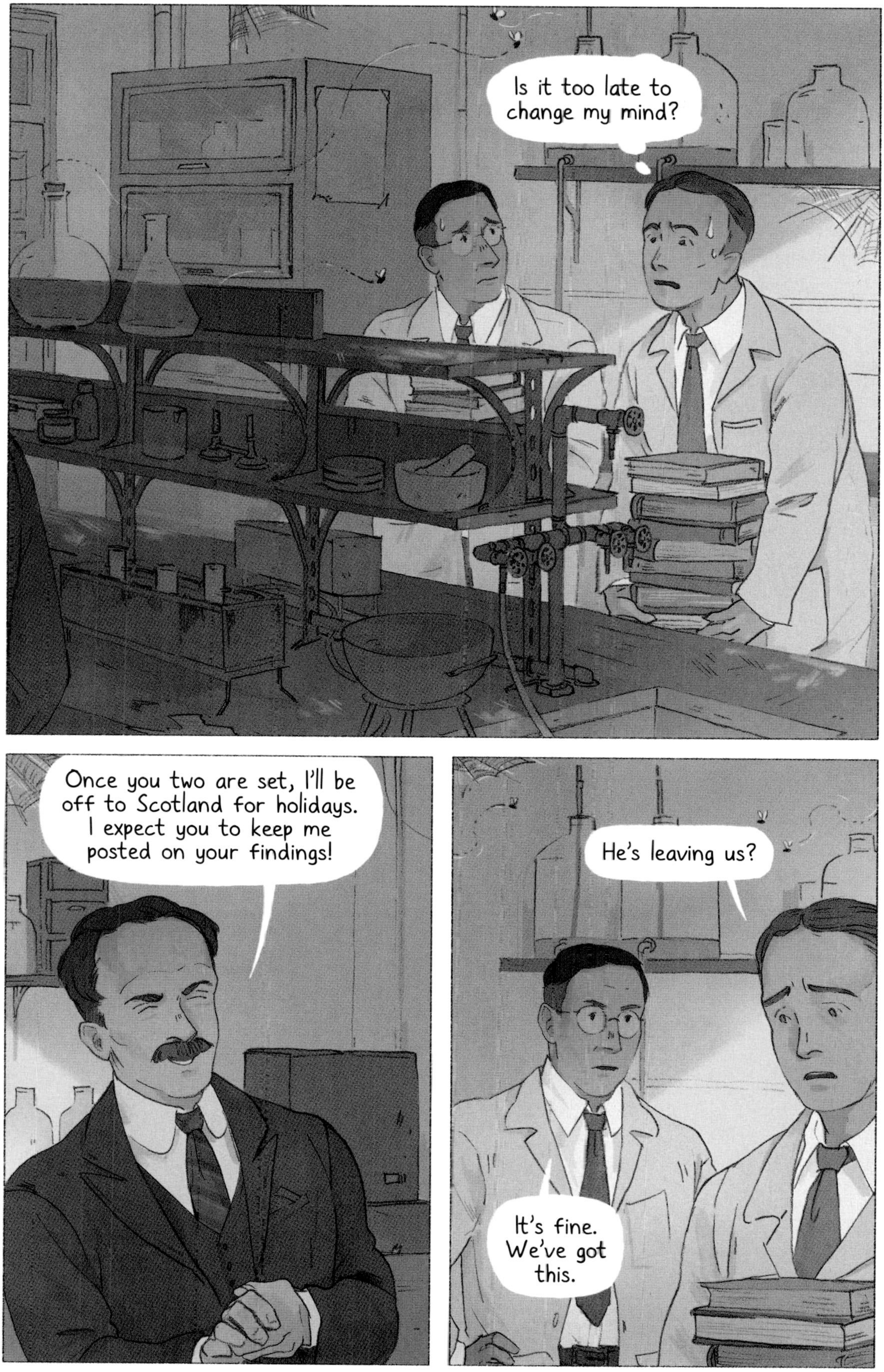
Is it too late to change my mind?
Once you two are set, I'll be off to Scotland for holidays. I expect you to keep me posted on your findings!
He's leaving us?
It's fine. We've got this.

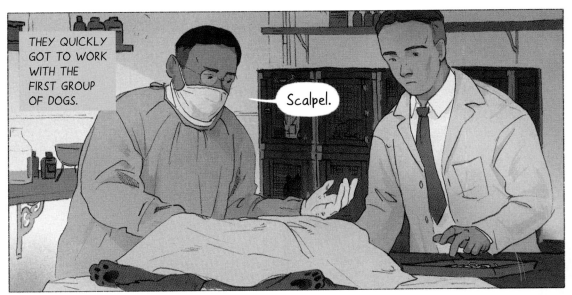

THEY QUICKLY GOT TO WORK WITH THE FIRST GROUP OF DOGS.

Scalpel.

Is that this little fellow's name?

They're not pets. They're lab animals. Researchers should never let themselves get emotionally attached. Don't you agree, Dr. Banting?

Yes, you're quite right. Very wise.

Dog 410

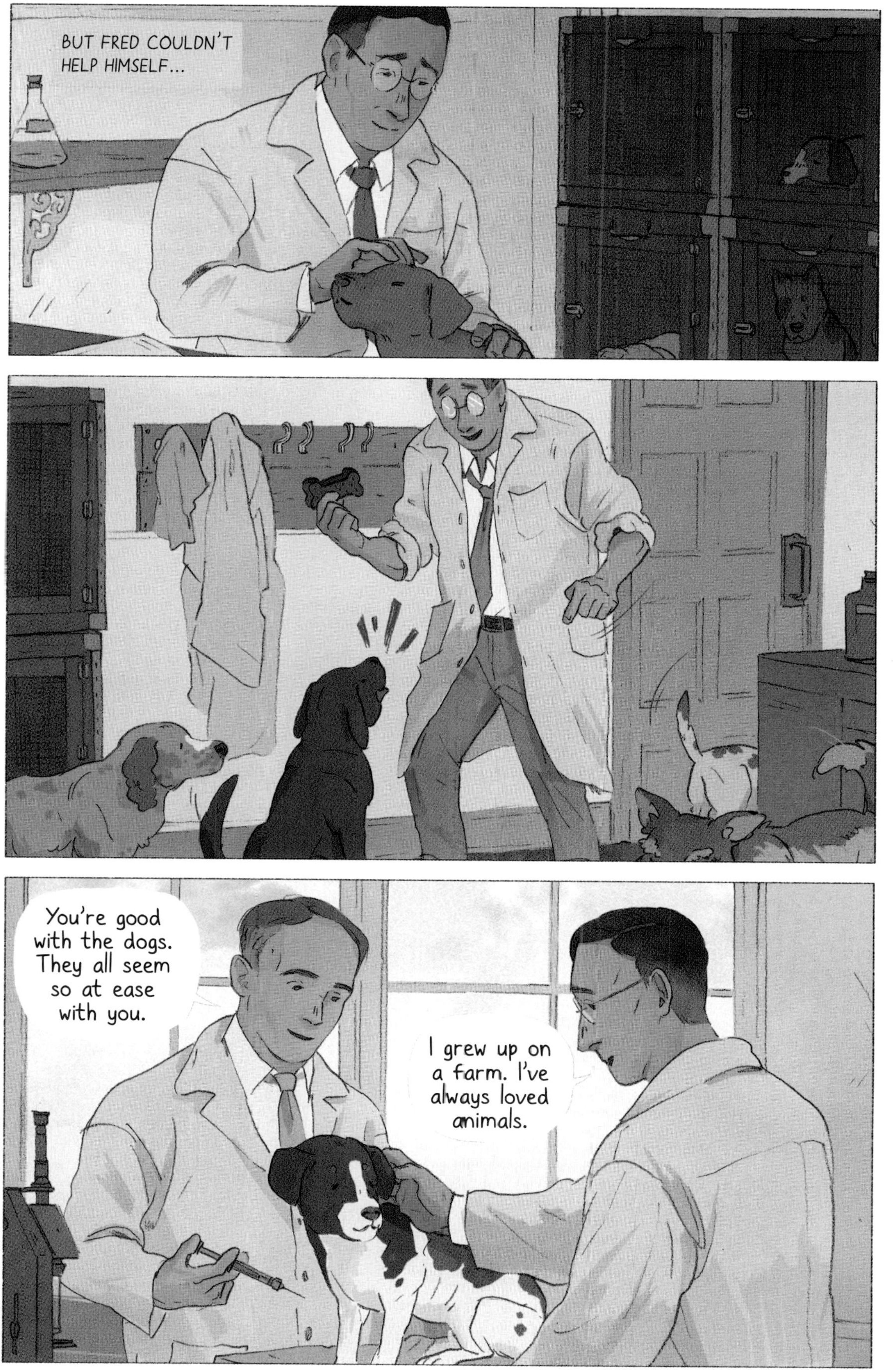
BUT FRED COULDN'T HELP HIMSELF...
You're good with the dogs. They all seem so at ease with you.
I grew up on a farm. I've always loved animals.

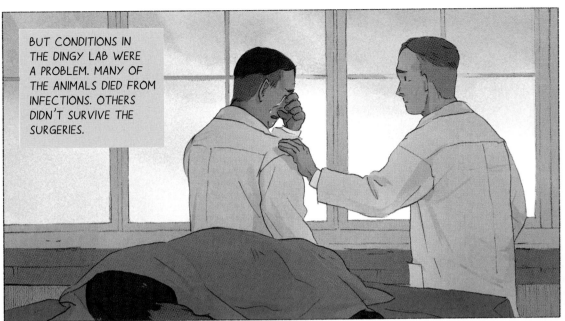

BUT CONDITIONS IN THE DINGY LAB WERE A PROBLEM. MANY OF THE ANIMALS DIED FROM INFECTIONS. OTHERS DIDN'T SURVIVE THE SURGERIES.

What do we do now?

We're just going to have to get some more dogs.

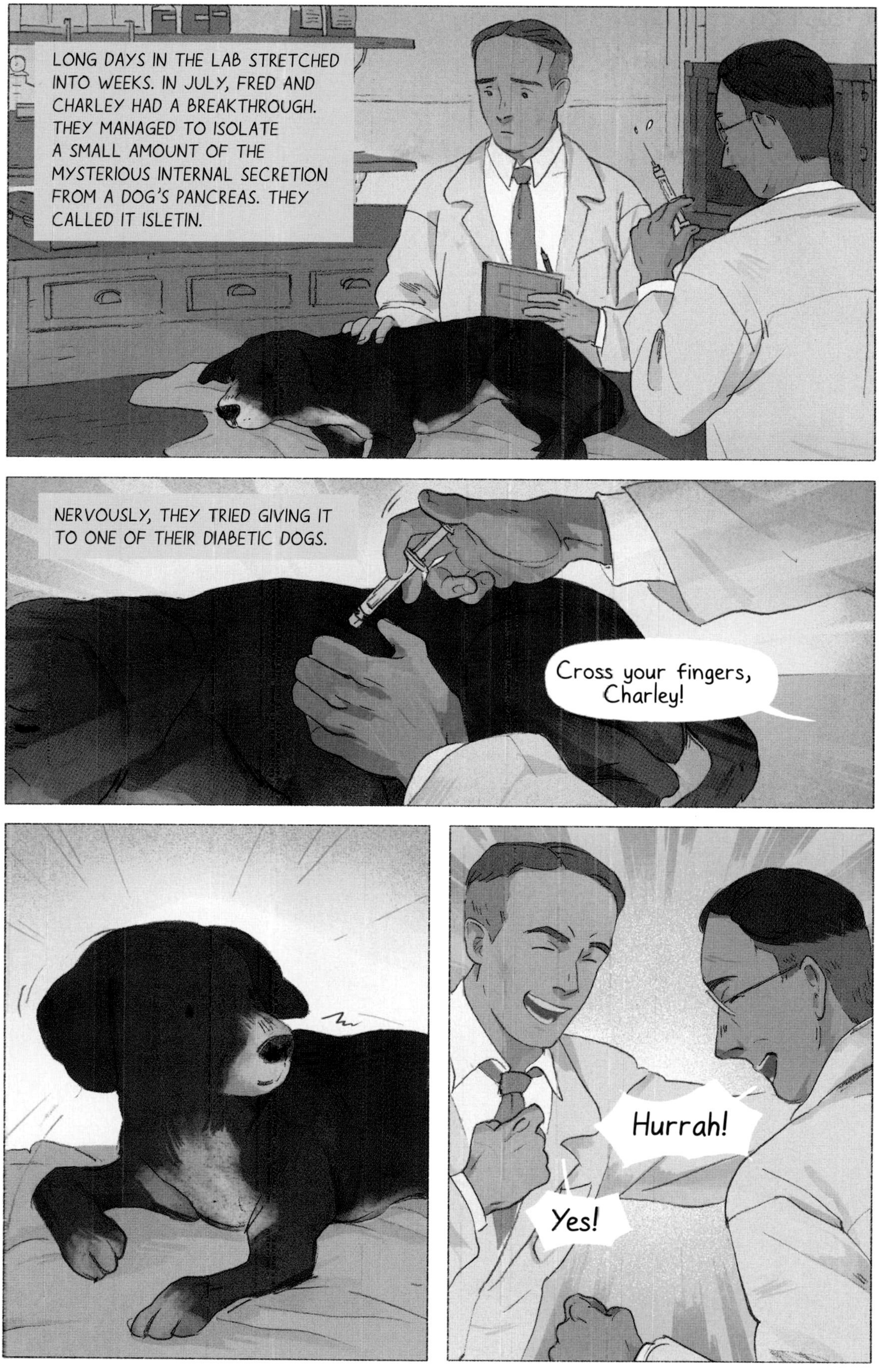
LONG DAYS IN THE LAB STRETCHED INTO WEEKS. IN JULY, FRED AND CHARLEY HAD A BREAKTHROUGH. THEY MANAGED TO ISOLATE A SMALL AMOUNT OF THE MYSTERIOUS INTERNAL SECRETION FROM A DOG'S PANCREAS. THEY CALLED IT ISLETIN.
NERVOUSLY, THEY TRIED GIVING IT TO ONE OF THEIR DIABETIC DOGS.
Cross your fingers, Charley!
Hurrah!
Yes!

THE ISLETIN SEEMED TO BE WORKING! BUT NOT AS WELL AS THEY'D HOPED. AND IT WAS TAKING FAR TOO LONG TO PRODUCE. FRED AND CHARLEY WERE ON THE RIGHT TRACK, BUT THERE WAS MUCH MORE WORK TO BE DONE.

Dear Professor Macleod,
I have so much to tell you …

WHILE CHARLEY TOOK SOME DAYS OFF TO TRAVEL AND VISIT FAMILY, FRED STAYED ON IN THE LAB. HE WAS DETERMINED TO PROVE THIS TREATMENT FOR DIABETES WOULD ONE DAY WORK ON HUMANS.

BUT IT WAS ALREADY AUGUST. PROFESSOR MACLEOD WOULD BE BACK IN A FEW WEEKS. TIME WAS RUNNING OUT.

FRED WORKED AROUND THE CLOCK.

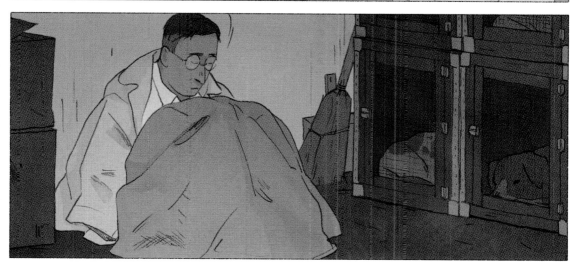

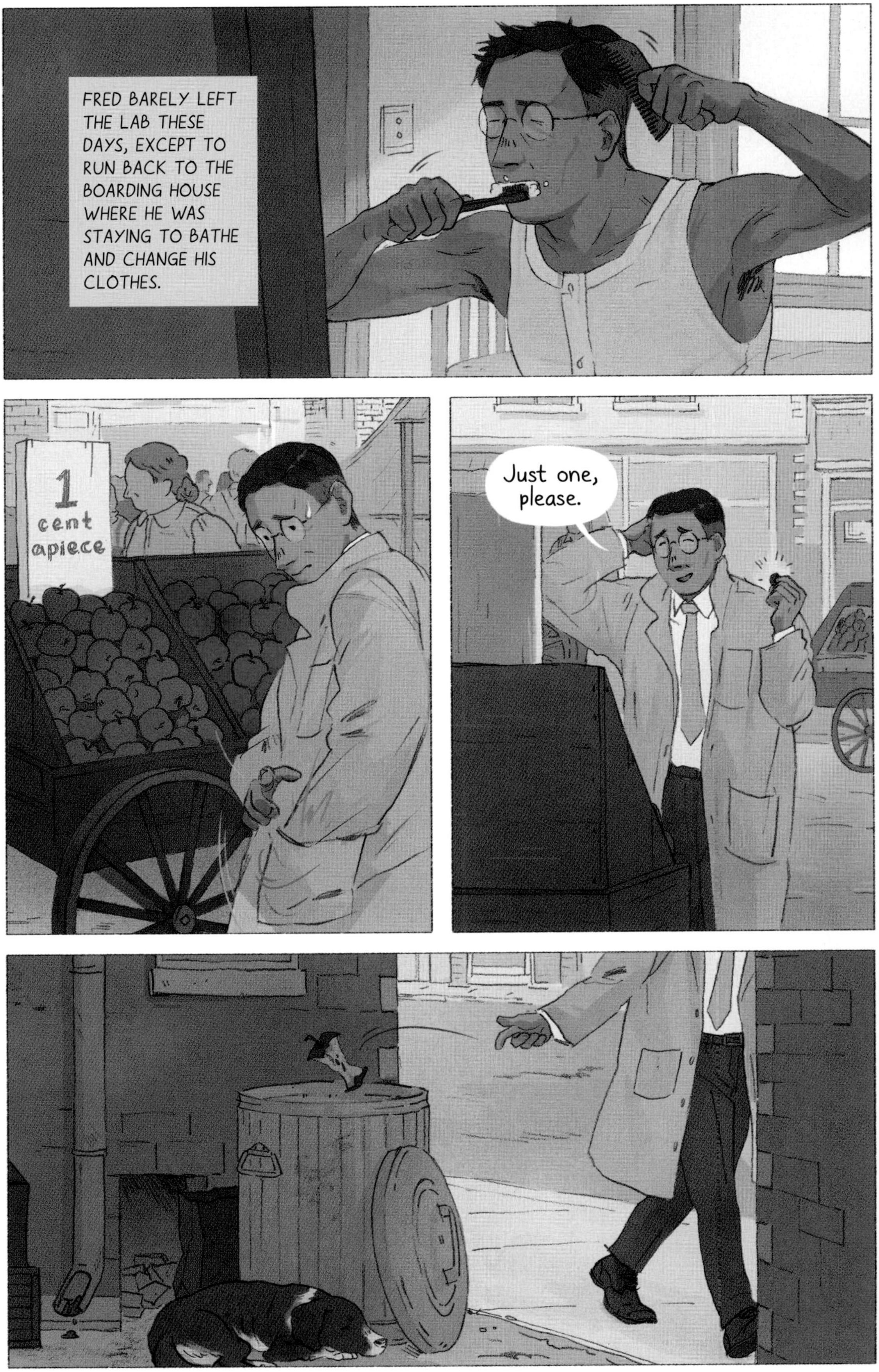
FRED BARELY LEFT THE LAB THESE DAYS, EXCEPT TO RUN BACK TO THE BOARDING HOUSE WHERE HE WAS STAYING TO BATHE AND CHANGE HIS CLOTHES.
1 cent apiece
Just one, please.

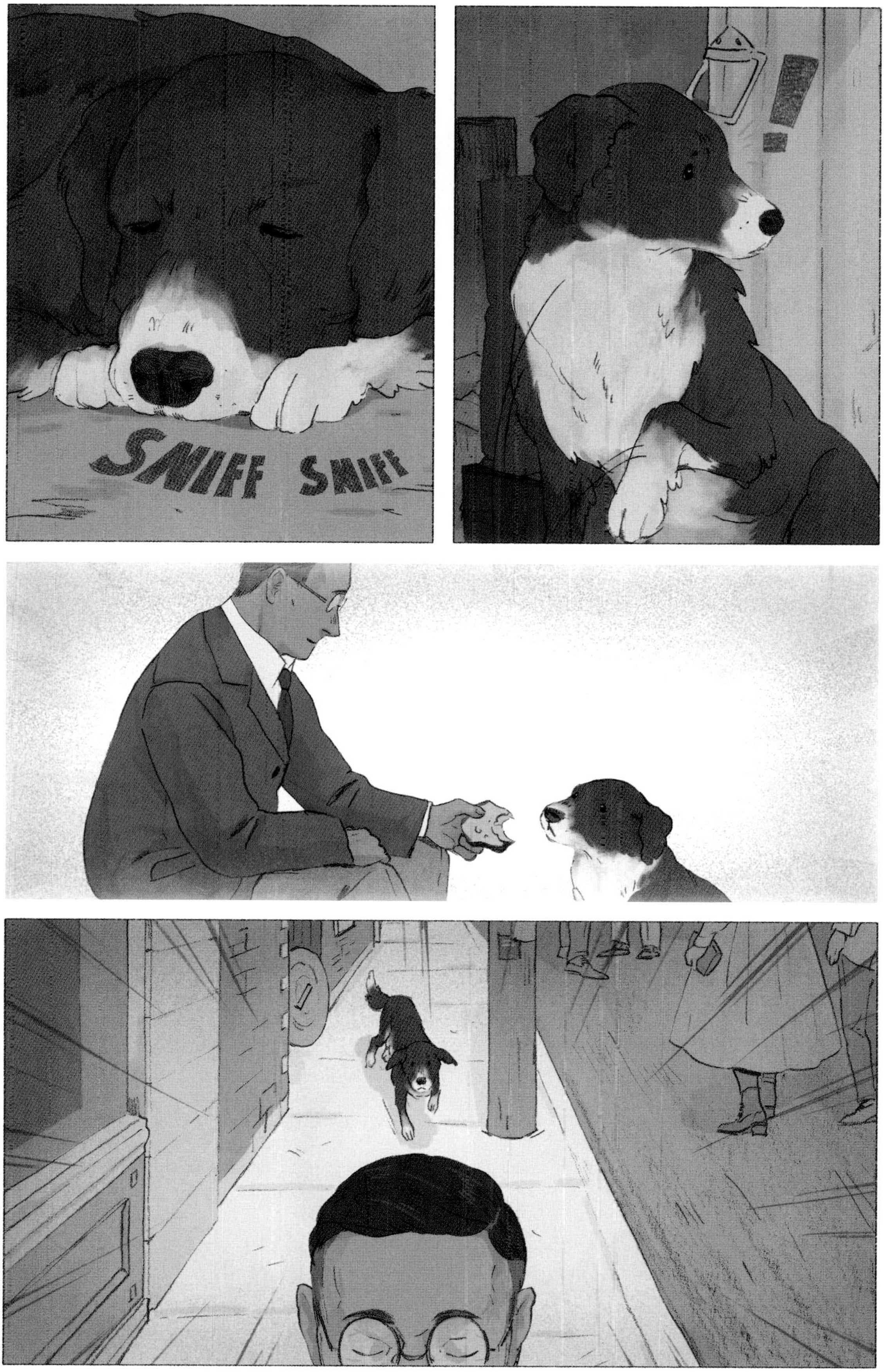
SNIFF SNIFF

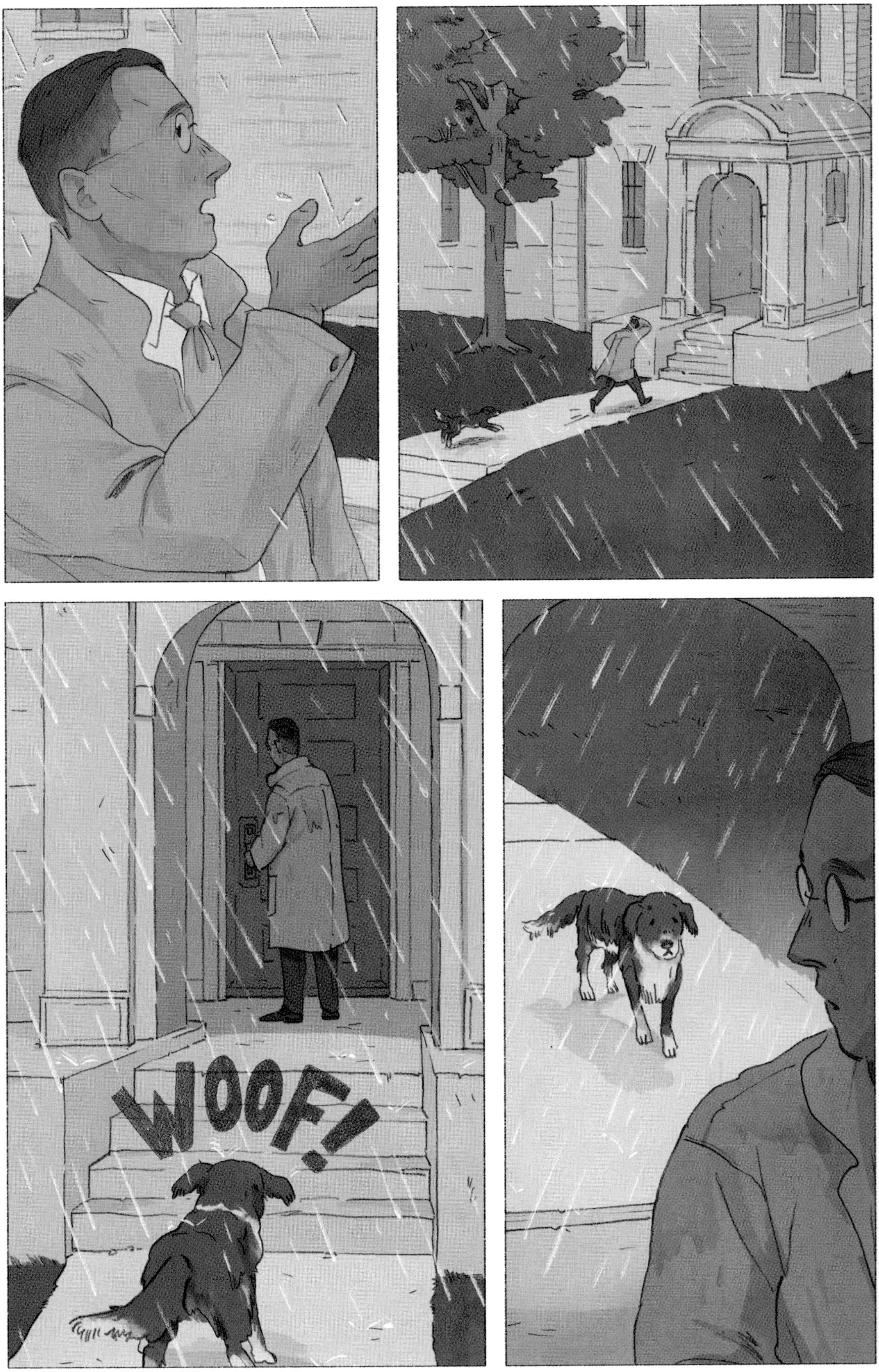
WOOF!

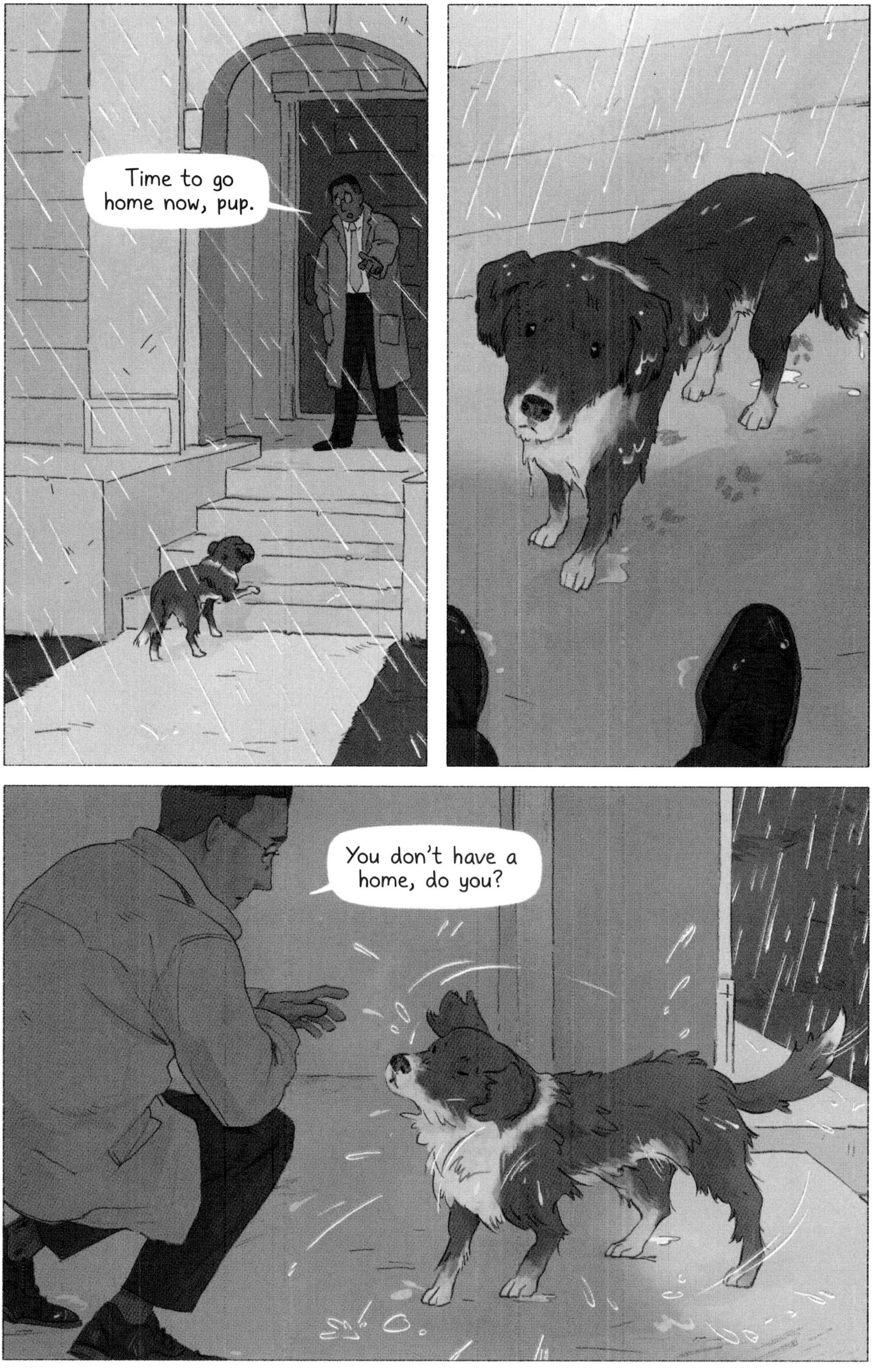
Time to go home now, pup.
You don't have a home, do you?

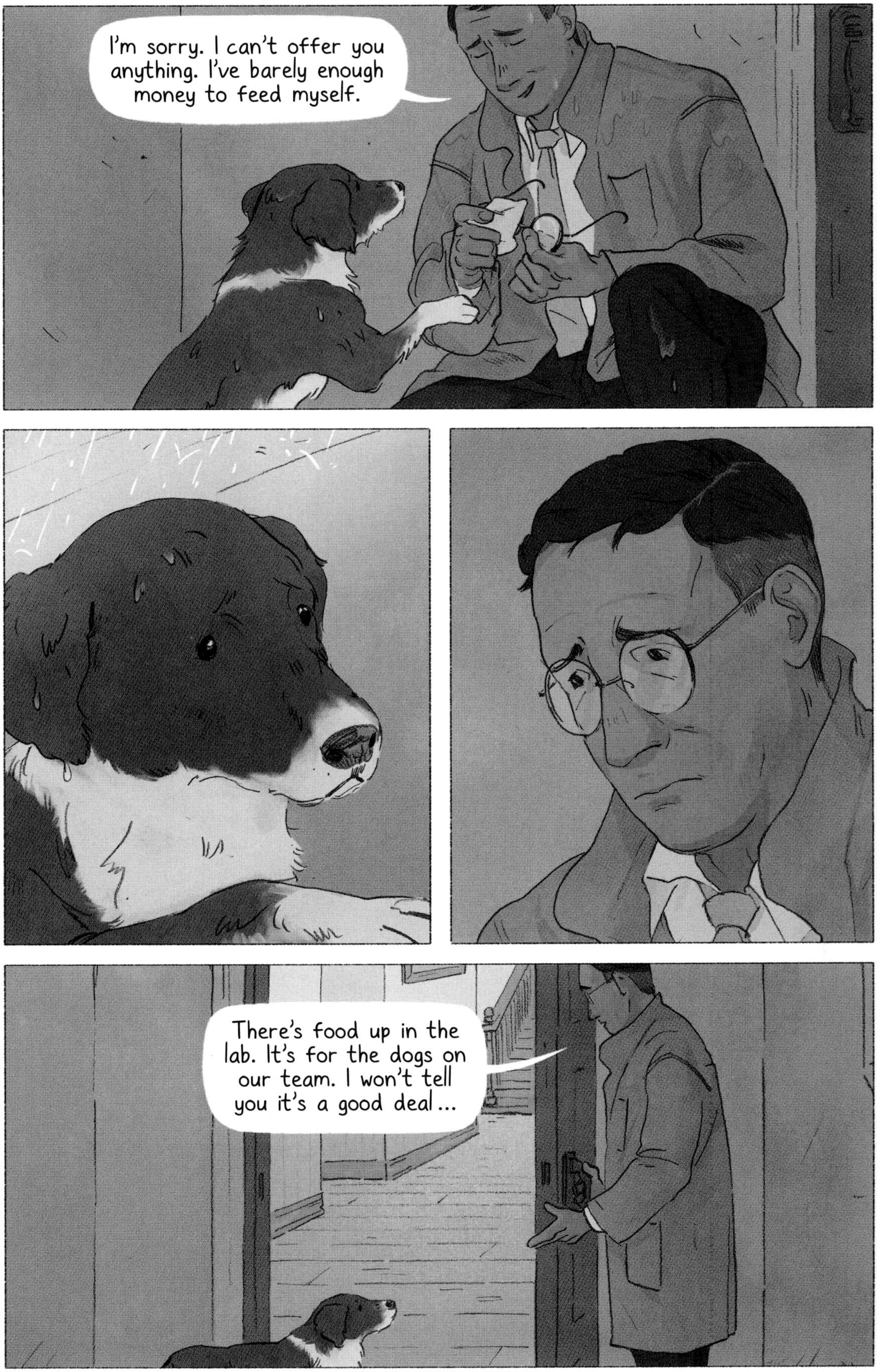
I'm sorry. I can't offer you anything. I've barely enough money to feed myself.
There's food up in the lab. It's for the dogs on our team. I won't tell you it's a good deal...

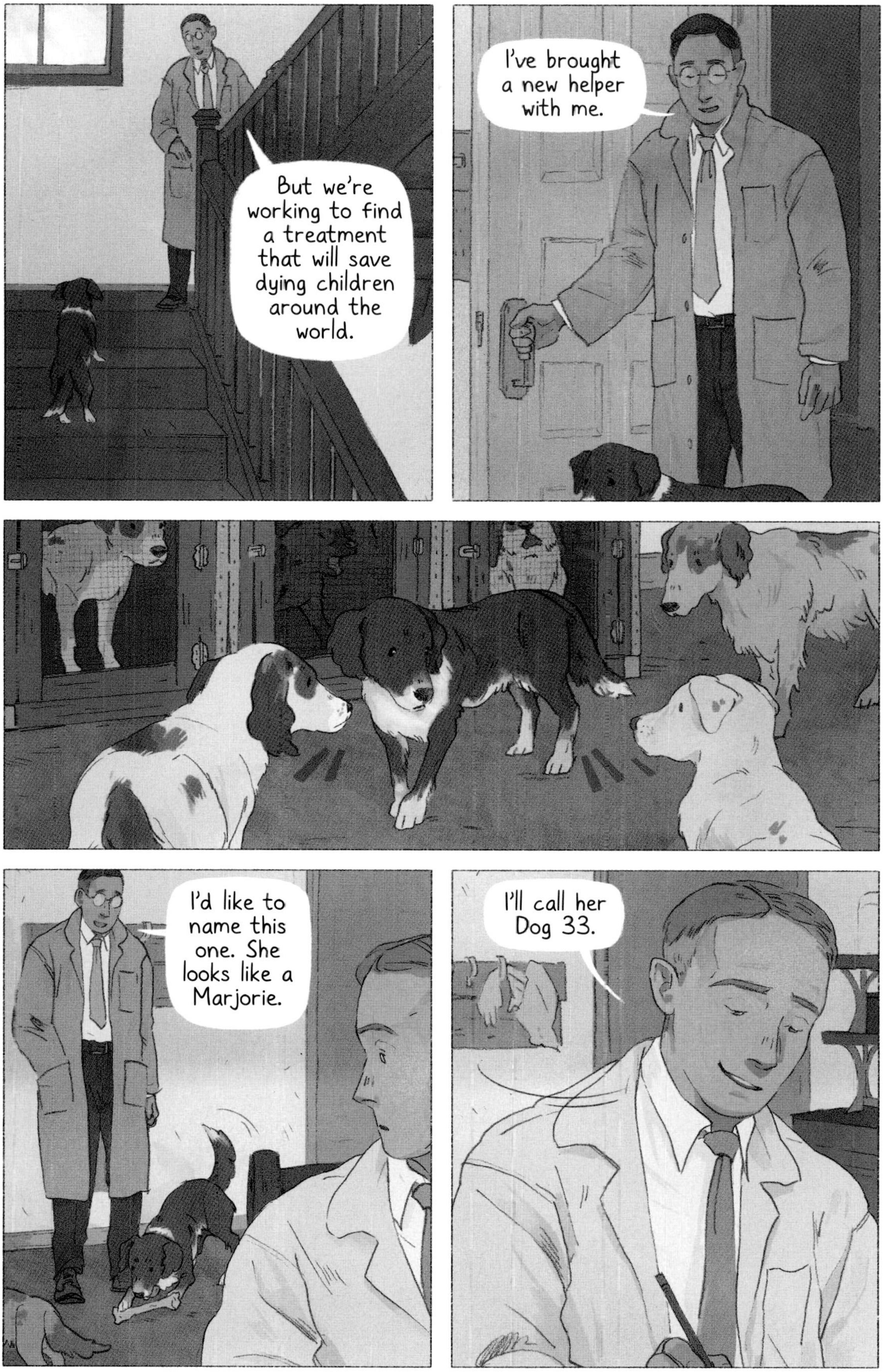
But we're working to find a treatment that will save dying children around the world.
I've brought a new helper with me.
I'd like to name this one. She looks like a Marjorie.
I'll call her Dog 33.

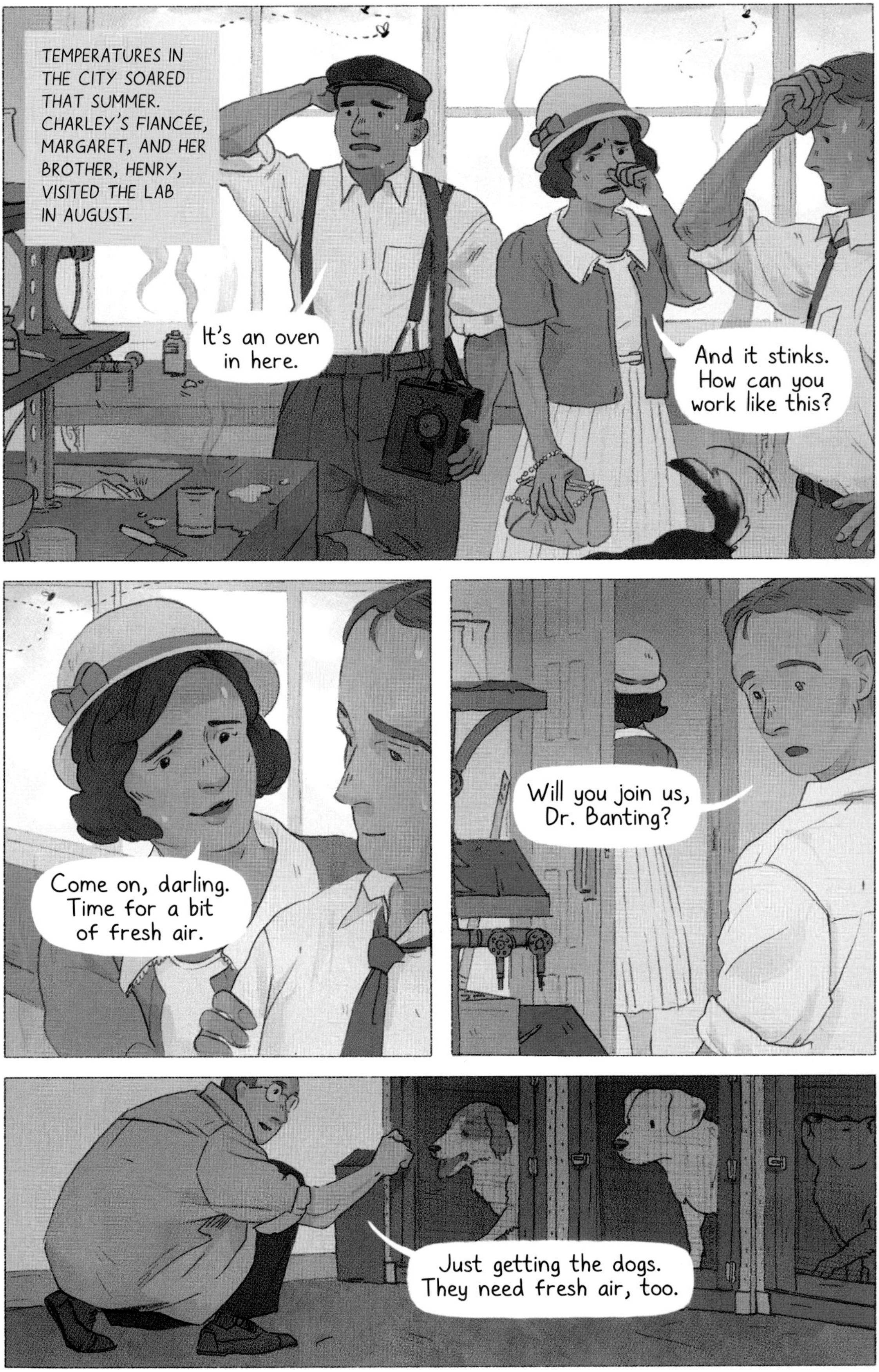
TEMPERATURES IN THE CITY SOARED THAT SUMMER. CHARLEY'S FIANCÉE, MARGARET, AND HER BROTHER, HENRY, VISITED THE LAB IN AUGUST.
It's an oven in here.
And it stinks. How can you work like this?
Come on, darling. Time for a bit of fresh air.
Will you join us, Dr. Banting?
Just getting the dogs. They need fresh air, too.

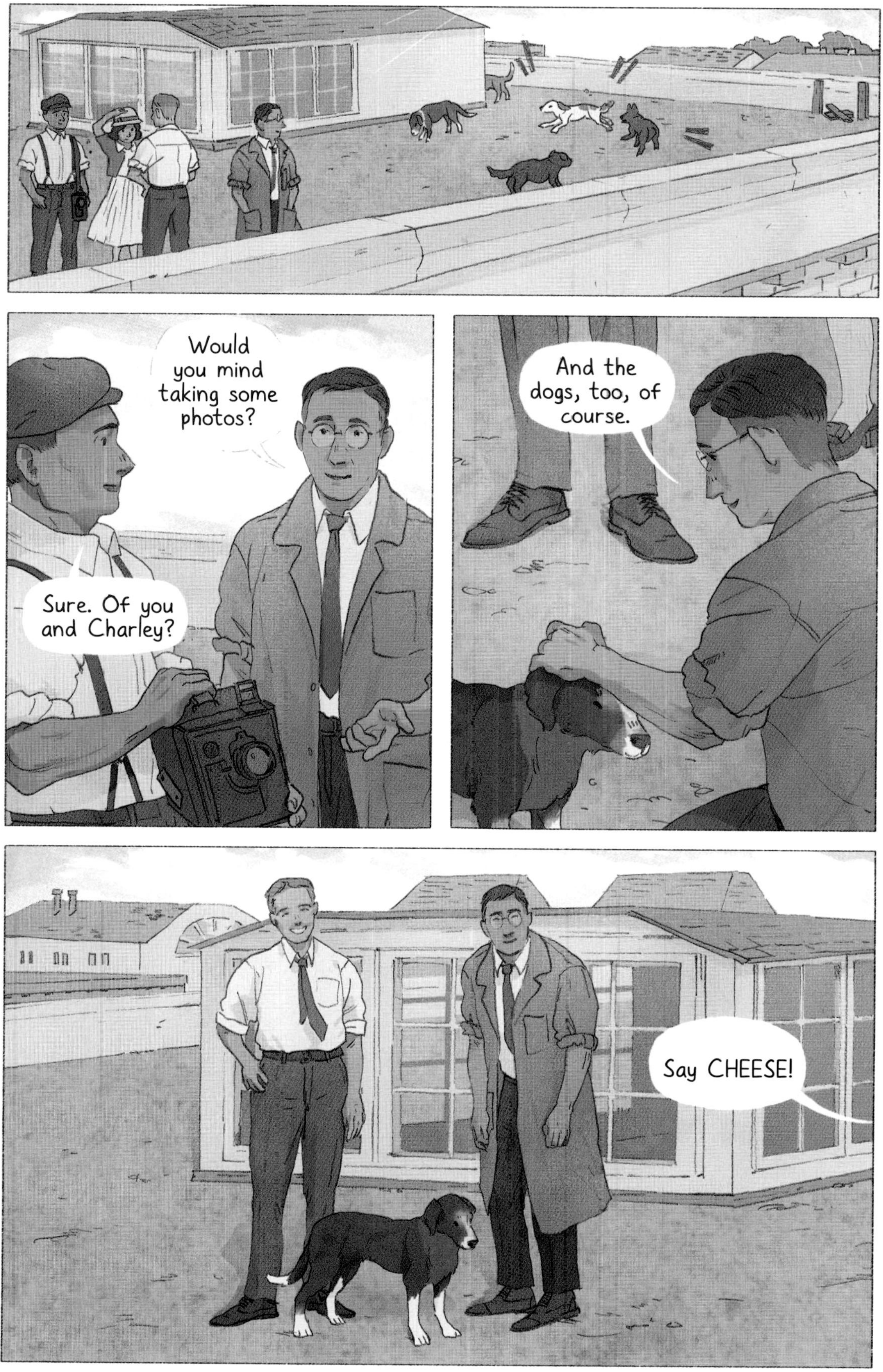

Would you mind taking some photos?
Sure. Of you and Charley?
And the dogs, too, of course.
Say CHEESE!

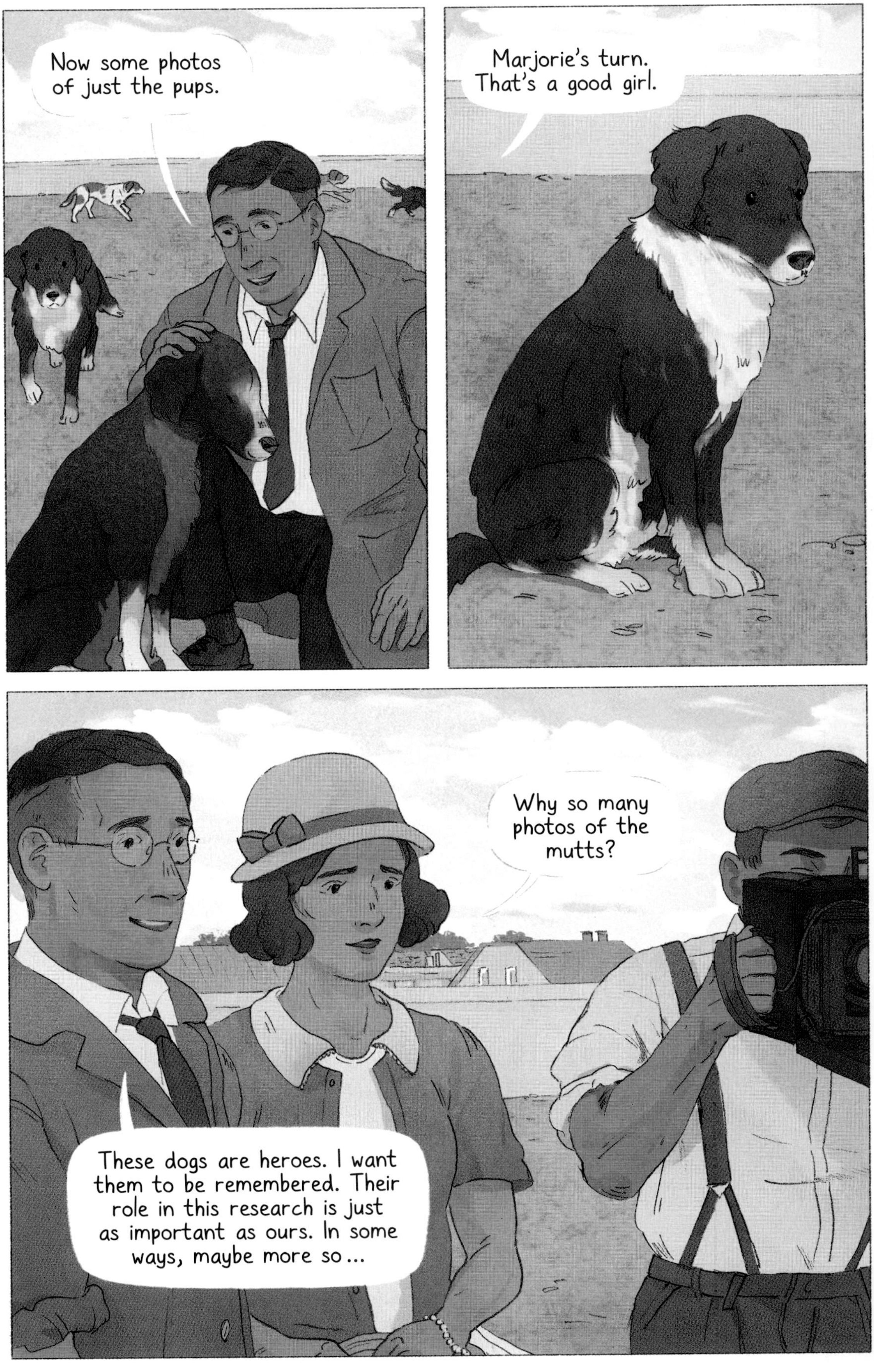

Now some photos of just the pups.
Marjorie's turn. That's a good girl.
Why so many photos of the mutts?
These dogs are heroes. I want them to be remembered. Their role in this research is just as important as ours. In some ways, maybe more so...

ON AUGUST 31, ANOTHER ONE OF THEIR LAB DOGS DIED—A COLLIE KNOWN ONLY AS DOG 92.

SHE HAD BEEN A SWEET DOG, AND HER LOSS WAS ESPECIALLY HEARTBREAKING FOR FRED.

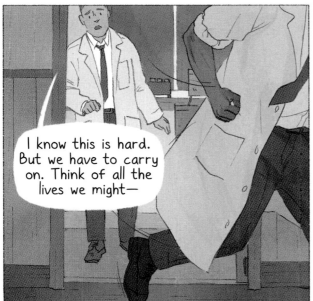

I know this is hard. But we have to carry on. Think of all the lives we might—

I-I need to be alone right now!

I'll never forget that dog as long as I live.

41

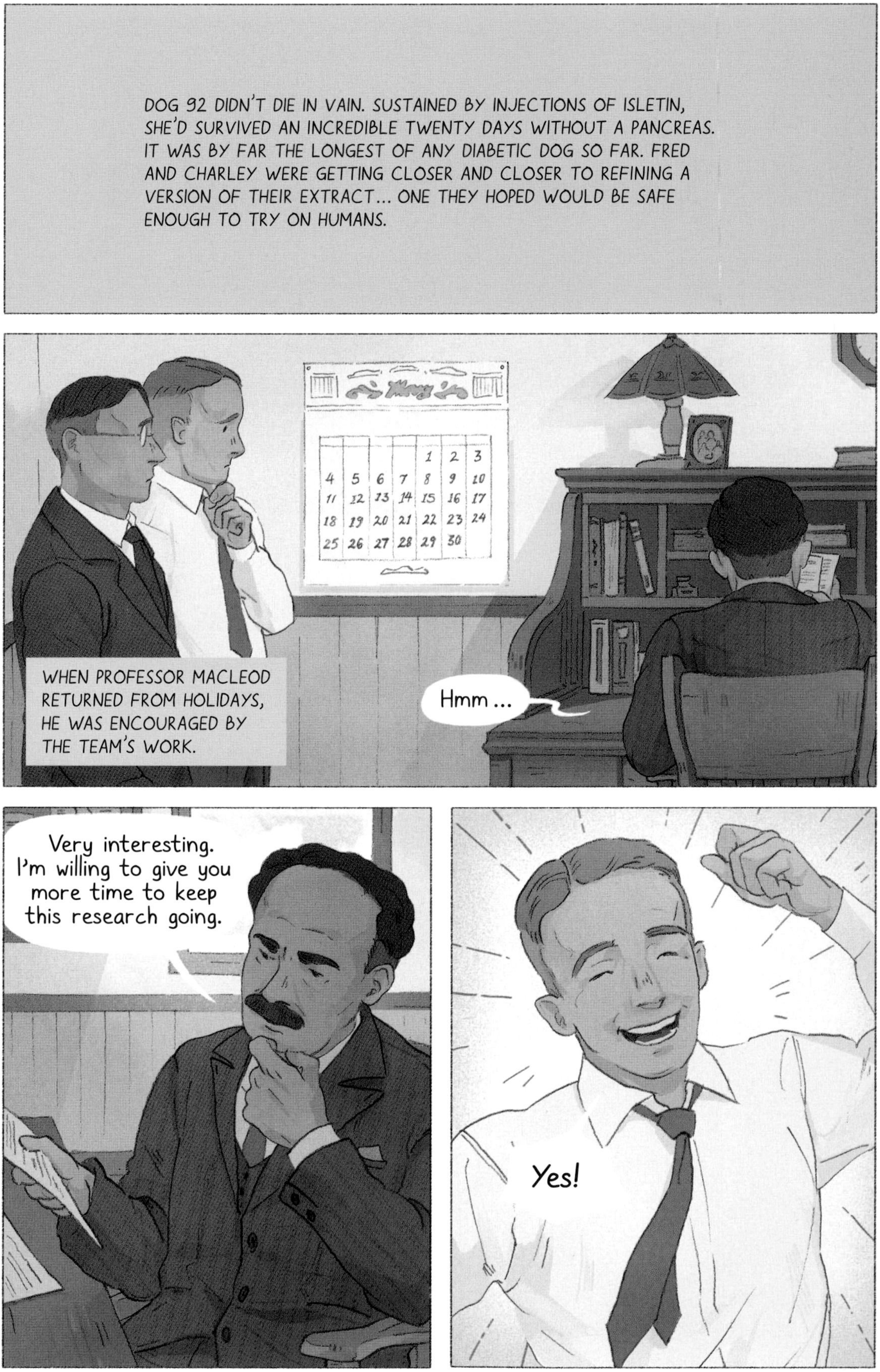
DOG 92 DIDN'T DIE IN VAIN. SUSTAINED BY INJECTIONS OF ISLETIN, SHE'D SURVIVED AN INCREDIBLE TWENTY DAYS WITHOUT A PANCREAS. IT WAS BY FAR THE LONGEST OF ANY DIABETIC DOG SO FAR. FRED AND CHARLEY WERE GETTING CLOSER AND CLOSER TO REFINING A VERSION OF THEIR EXTRACT... ONE THEY HOPED WOULD BE SAFE ENOUGH TO TRY ON HUMANS.
WHEN PROFESSOR MACLEOD RETURNED FROM HOLIDAYS, HE WAS ENCOURAGED BY THE TEAM'S WORK.
Hmm...
Very interesting. I'm willing to give you more time to keep this research going.
Yes!

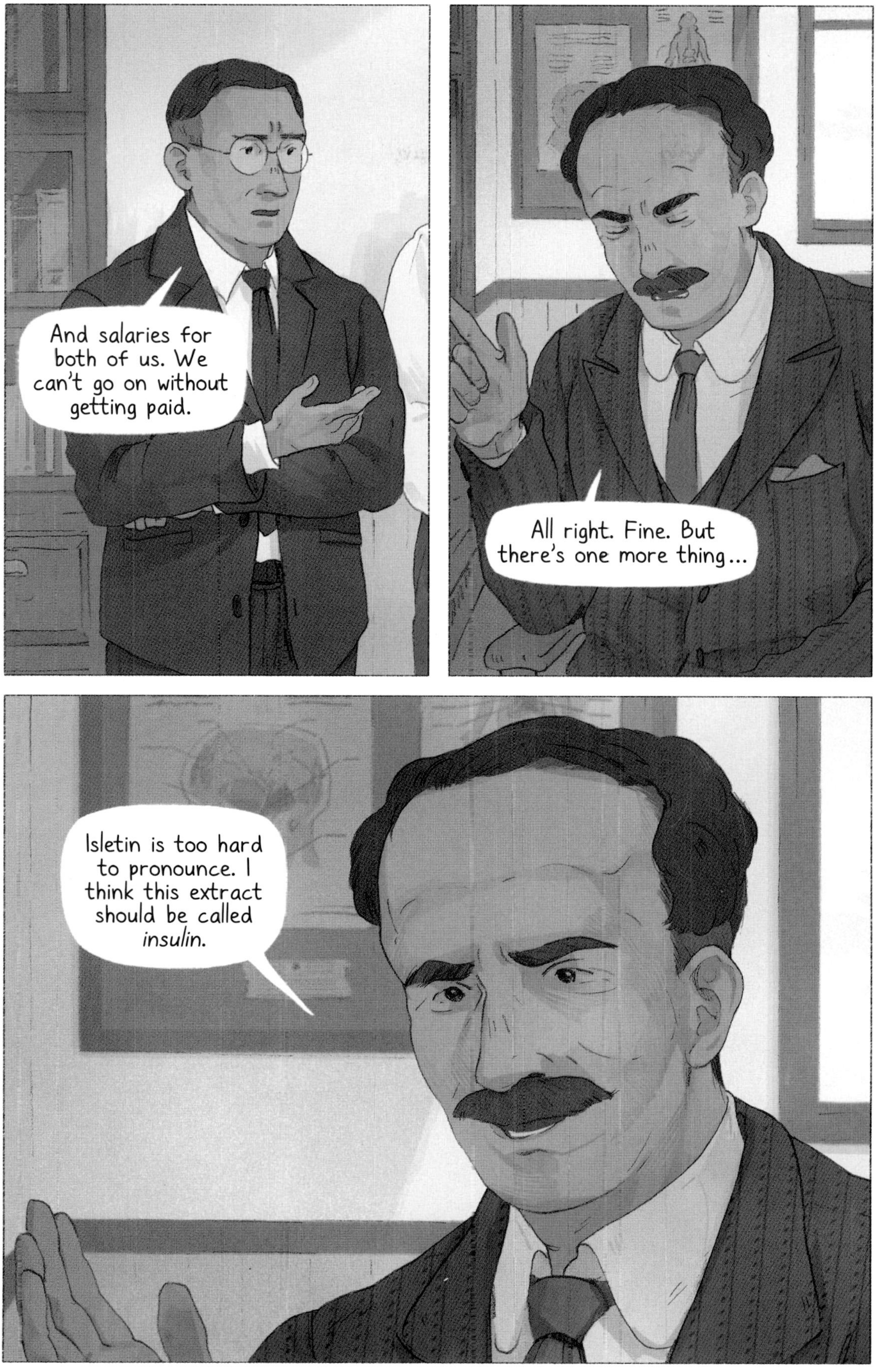
And salaries for both of us. We can't go on without getting paid.
All right. Fine. But there's one more thing...
Isletin is too hard to pronounce. I think this extract should be called *insulin*.

OVER THE NEXT FEW MONTHS, FRED AND CHARLEY CONTINUED TO REFINE THEIR EXTRACT, WHILE AT THE SAME TIME LOOKING FOR BETTER WAYS TO PRODUCE IT. FRED HAD THE IDEA OF SALVAGING COW PANCREASES FROM SLAUGHTERHOUSES. THE ORGANS WERE EASY TO FIND, AND USING THEM SPARED SOME OF THEIR DOGS FROM SURGERY.

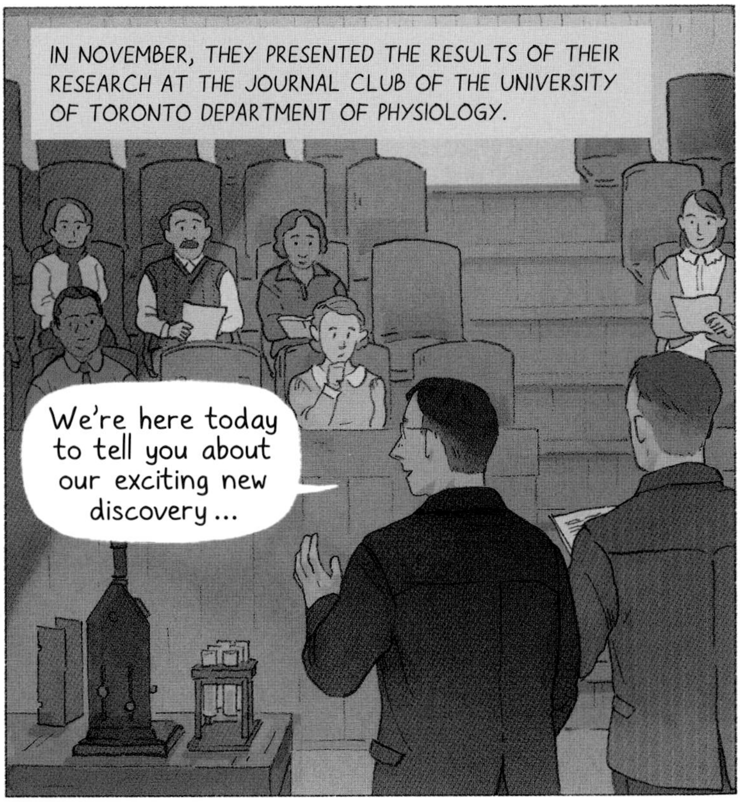
IN NOVEMBER, THEY PRESENTED THE RESULTS OF THEIR RESEARCH AT THE JOURNAL CLUB OF THE UNIVERSITY OF TORONTO DEPARTMENT OF PHYSIOLOGY.
We're here today to tell you about our exciting new discovery ...

NEWS OF THEIR RESEARCH BUZZED THROUGH THE MEDICAL COMMUNITY. PEOPLE WERE HOPEFUL BUT SKEPTICAL. THEY WANTED MORE PROOF THAT THIS WAS REALLY THE BREAKTHROUGH FRED AND CHARLEY CLAIMED IT TO BE.

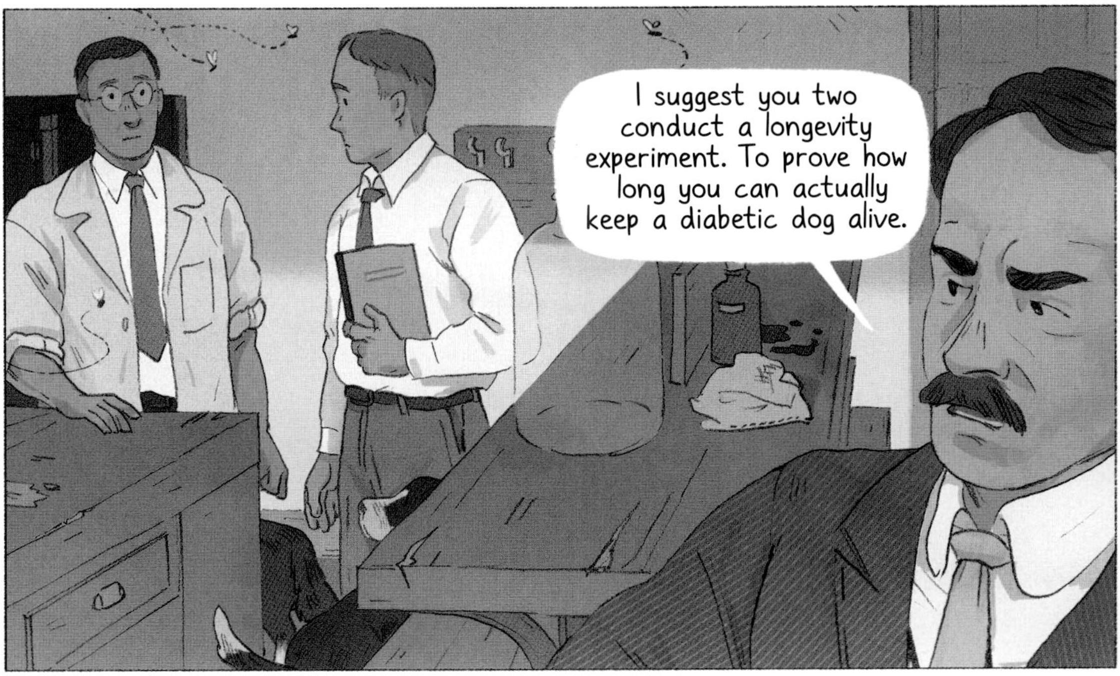
I suggest you two conduct a longevity experiment. To prove how long you can actually keep a diabetic dog alive.

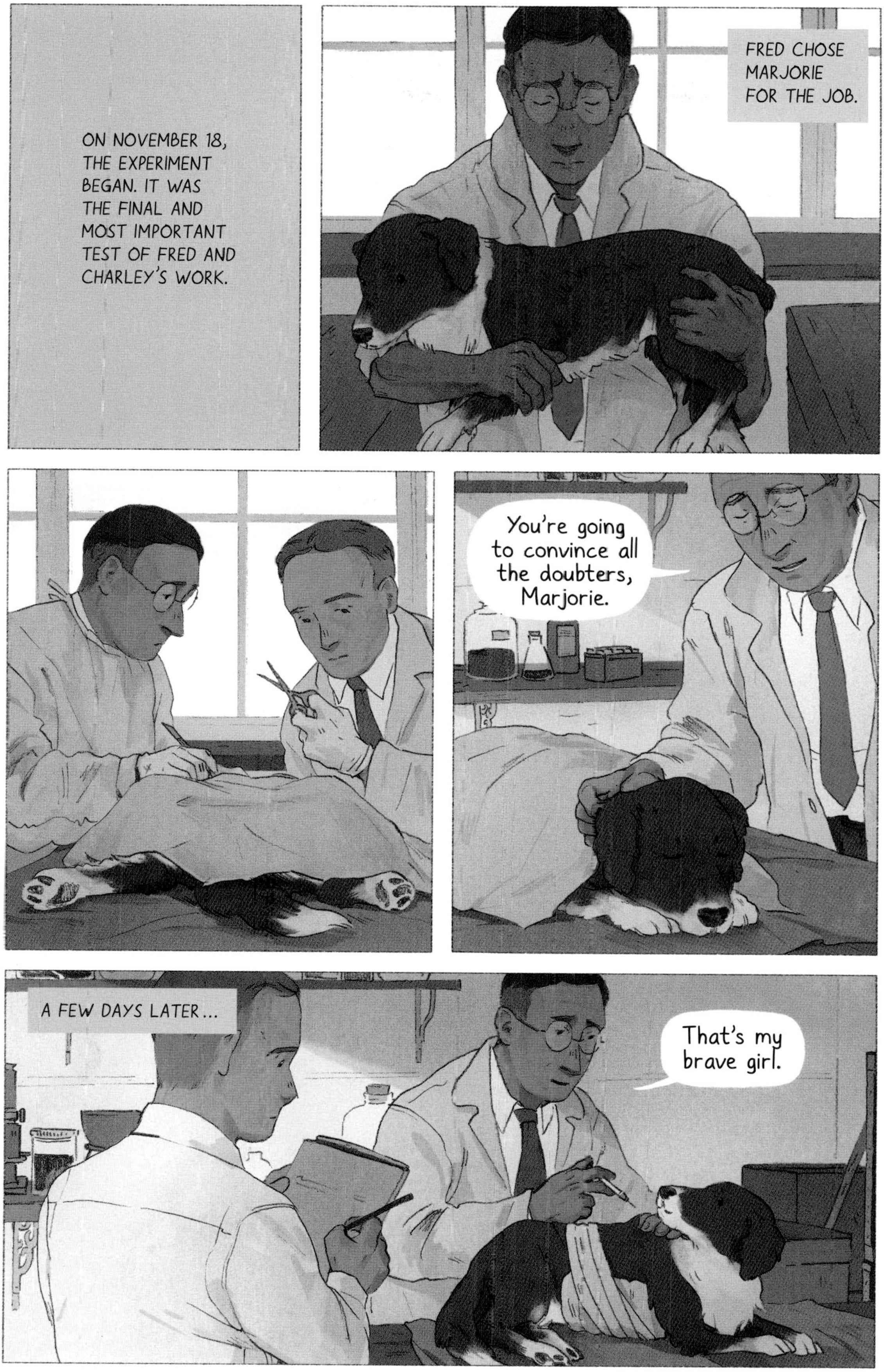
ON NOVEMBER 18, THE EXPERIMENT BEGAN. IT WAS THE FINAL AND MOST IMPORTANT TEST OF FRED AND CHARLEY'S WORK.
FRED CHOSE MARJORIE FOR THE JOB.
You're going to convince all the doubters, Marjorie.
A FEW DAYS LATER...
That's my brave girl.

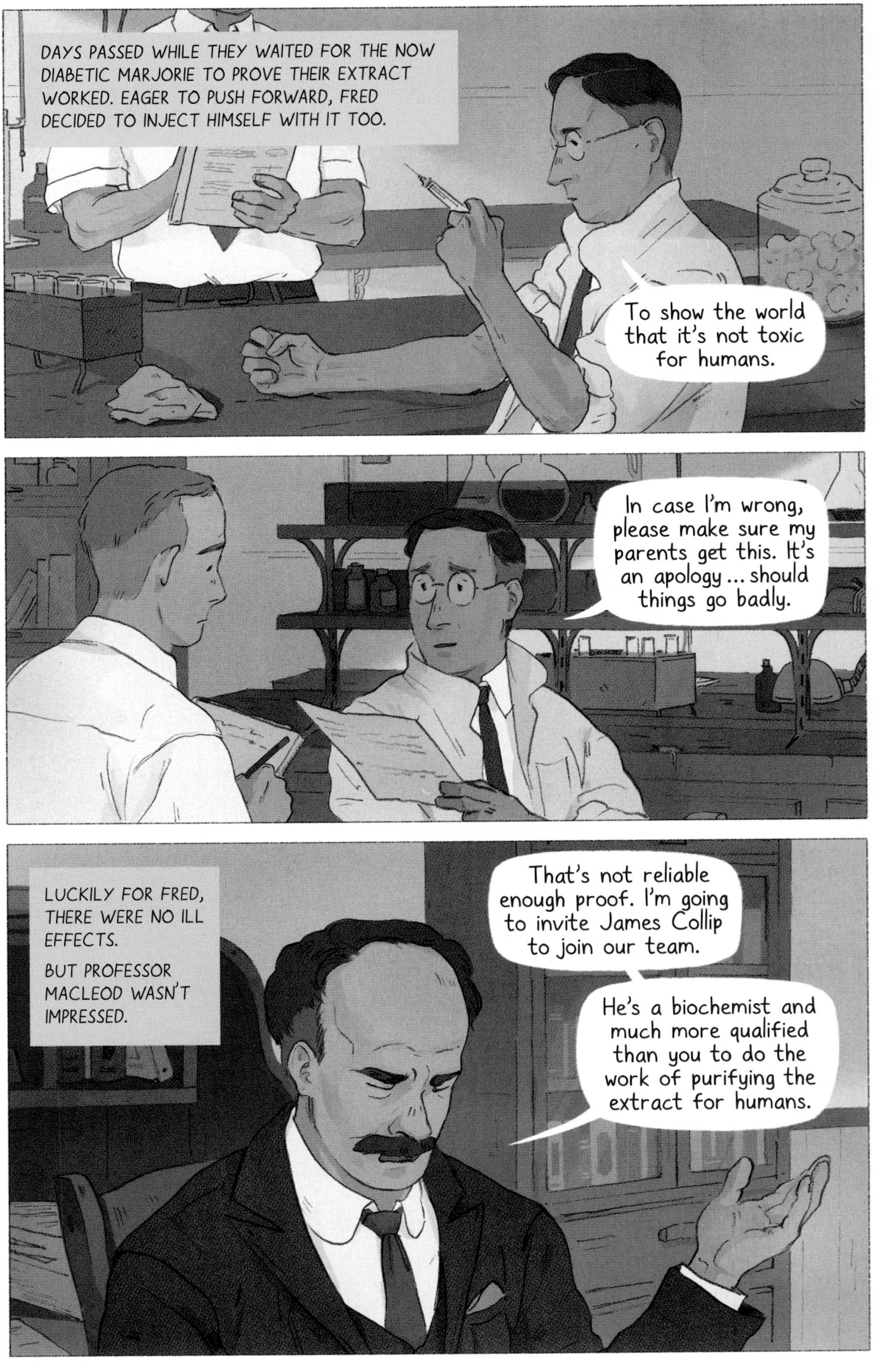
DAYS PASSED WHILE THEY WAITED FOR THE NOW DIABETIC MARJORIE TO PROVE THEIR EXTRACT WORKED. EAGER TO PUSH FORWARD, FRED DECIDED TO INJECT HIMSELF WITH IT TOO.
To show the world that it's not toxic for humans.
In case I'm wrong, please make sure my parents get this. It's an apology ... should things go badly.
LUCKILY FOR FRED, THERE WERE NO ILL EFFECTS.
BUT PROFESSOR MACLEOD WASN'T IMPRESSED.
That's not reliable enough proof. I'm going to invite James Collip to join our team.
He's a biochemist and much more qualified than you to do the work of purifying the extract for humans.

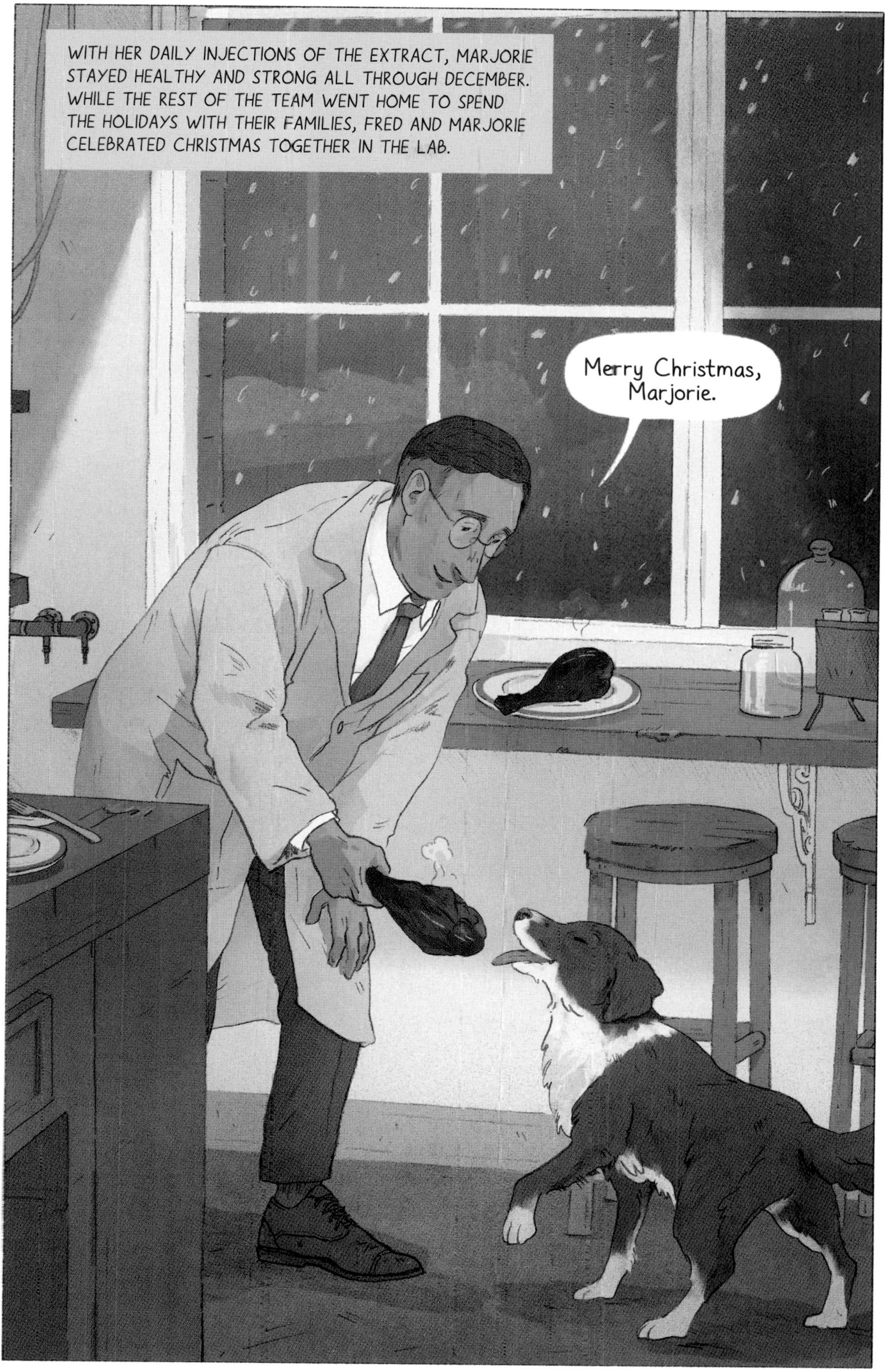
WITH HER DAILY INJECTIONS OF THE EXTRACT, MARJORIE STAYED HEALTHY AND STRONG ALL THROUGH DECEMBER. WHILE THE REST OF THE TEAM WENT HOME TO SPEND THE HOLIDAYS WITH THEIR FAMILIES, FRED AND MARJORIE CELEBRATED CHRISTMAS TOGETHER IN THE LAB.
Merry Christmas, Marjorie.

NEARING THE END OF JANUARY 1922, MARJORIE HAD SURVIVED FOR ALMOST SEVENTY DAYS WITHOUT A PANCREAS. IN FRED'S OPINION, IT WAS THE PROOF THE MEDICAL WORLD HAD ASKED FOR.

IT WAS NOW TIME TO TRY THEIR EXTRACT ON A HUMAN PATIENT.

BUT THERE WASN'T ENOUGH SUPPLY TO KEEP A STRAY DOG ALIVE ANY LONGER. IT WAS IMPORTANT TO USE WHAT LITTLE THEY HAD FOR A CHILD WITH DIABETES.

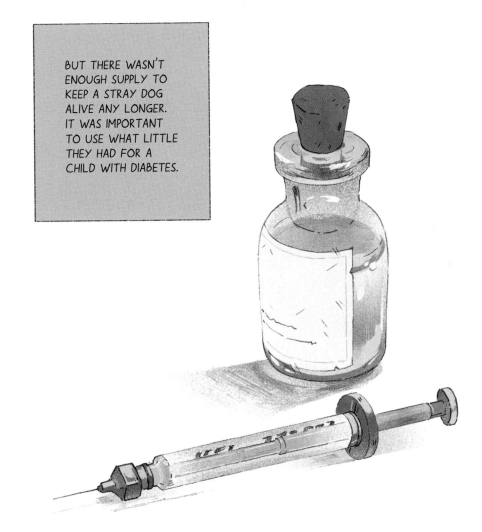

MARJORIE'S WORK WAS DONE.

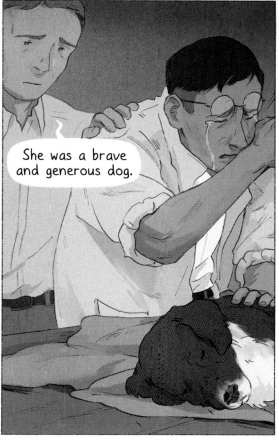

She was a brave and generous dog.

I'm sorry I couldn't offer you anything better. But one day, the children you helped to save will hear your story and know your name.

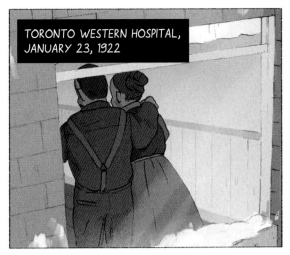

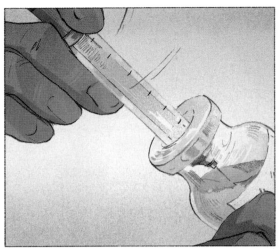

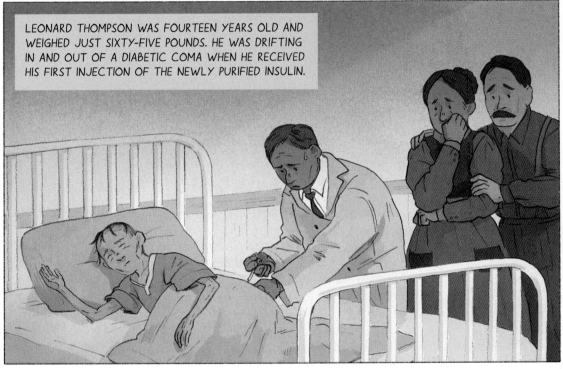

TORONTO WESTERN HOSPITAL, JANUARY 23, 1922
LEONARD THOMPSON WAS FOURTEEN YEARS OLD AND WEIGHED JUST SIXTY-FIVE POUNDS. HE WAS DRIFTING IN AND OUT OF A DIABETIC COMA WHEN HE RECEIVED HIS FIRST INJECTION OF THE NEWLY PURIFIED INSULIN.

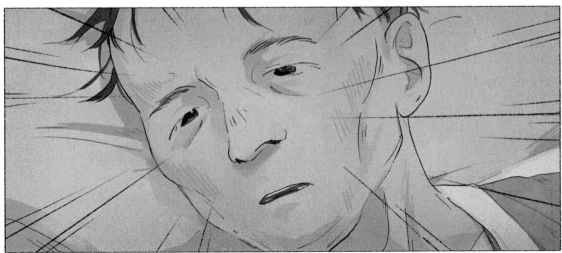

THE EFFECTS WERE PRACTICALLY MIRACULOUS. LEONARD BEGAN TO IMPROVE ALMOST IMMEDIATELY.

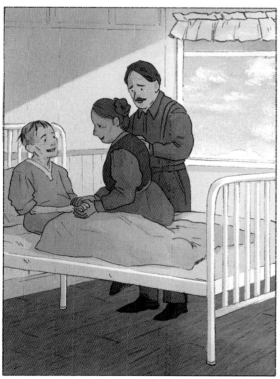

EAGER TO GET INSULIN INTO THE HANDS OF AILING PATIENTS AS SOON AS POSSIBLE, THE TEAM SOLD THEIR RIGHTS TO THE LIFE-SAVING TREATMENT TO THE UNIVERSITY OF TORONTO FOR ONE DOLLAR EACH.

AS FRED FAMOUSLY SAID: "INSULIN DOES NOT BELONG TO ME. IT BELONGS TO THE WORLD."

AUTHOR'S NOTE

AN ANCIENT DISEASE

Throughout history, type 1 diabetes, formerly known as juvenile diabetes, was a death sentence for millions of people around the world, most of them children and young adults. Symptoms of the disease were first recorded in or around 1550 BCE by ancient Egyptian healers. In the thousands of years that have since passed, no cure has ever been discovered.

Type 1 diabetes (T1D) is an autoimmune disease that attacks the pancreas, affecting the organ's ability to produce insulin—the essential hormone that regulates the level of sugar in our blood. Without insulin, blood sugar builds up to dangerous levels, causing serious health complications and eventually death. Although T1D can strike at any age, it is most often diagnosed in children between four and seven, and in adolescents between ten and fourteen. The exact cause of T1D remains unknown.

Until 1921, doctors had no way to treat diabetes except by restricting food intake to keep blood sugar levels down. For many patients, that meant a slow, agonizing death by starvation. But in May of that year, a penniless doctor, a student assistant, and a pack of Toronto street dogs set out to change that forever.

THE STORY

Frederick Banting and Charles Best conducted their research in a small laboratory on the top floor of the University of Toronto's medical building. Their test subjects were dogs. Banting and Best made half the animals diabetic by surgically removing their pancreases. They then extracted the mysterious pancreatic

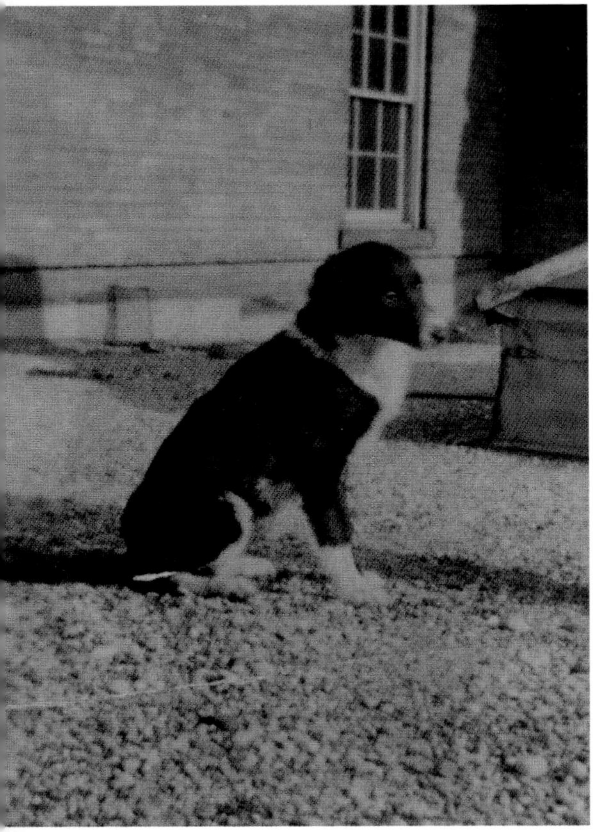

DOG 33, ALSO KNOWN AS MARJORIE

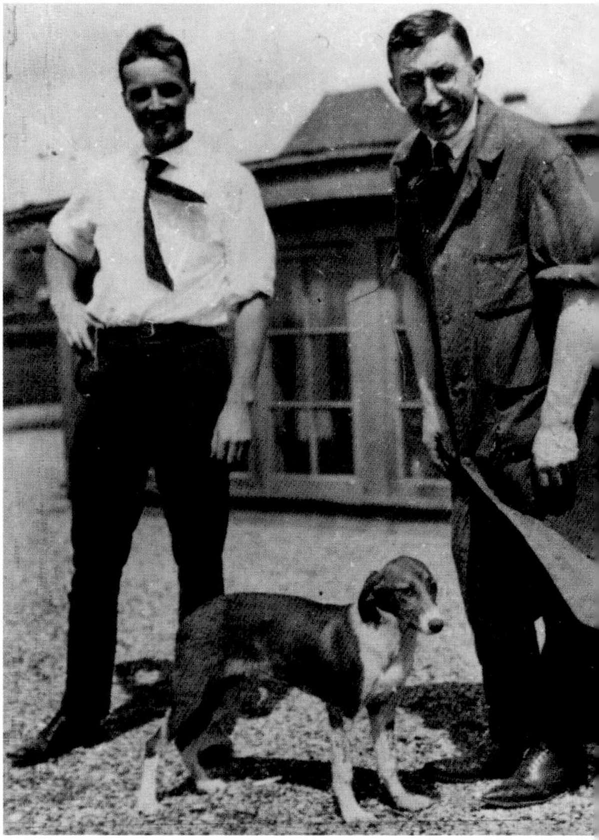

CHARLES BEST AND FREDERICK BANTING WITH DOG 408

secretion from the remaining dogs in the hopes of using it to keep the diabetic ones alive. This extraction was a primitive version of today's insulin. Under the direction of Professor J. J. R. Macleod, and with the help of biochemist James B. Collip, they were able to produce a refined version for use on human patients.

Fred and Charley were both young and inexperienced in a laboratory. Their methods were somewhat haphazard, their research notes spotty, and their later recall of specific details patchy. This resulted in some gaps in the narrative. My retelling of Fred's story is based mainly on firsthand accounts as they were recorded at the time and remembered years later, although some parts of the timeline were condensed in the interest of pacing.

Like the rest of the insulin dogs, Marjorie was a stray. Nothing is known about her life before she met Dr. Banting. Those parts of this book have been imagined. But her important role in the discovery of insulin is real. Marjorie was the dog who ultimately survived the longest on Banting and Best's treatment, proving to the medical world that insulin was ready to move forward into human trials. She's been called "the most important dog in the world."

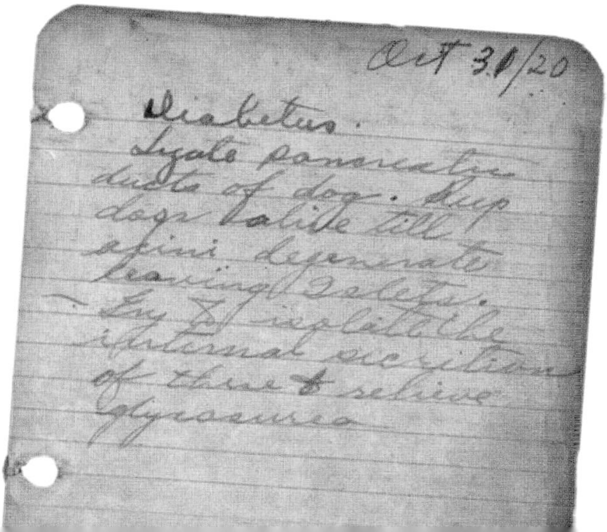

Oct 31/20
Diabetus.
Ligate pancreatic
ducts of dog. Keep
dogs alive till
acini degenerate
leaving Islets.
Try to isolate the
internal secretion
of these to relieve
glycosurea

BANTING'S MIDDLE-OF-THE-NIGHT NOTE DESCRIBING HIS IDEA FOR A TREATMENT FOR DIABETES

AN ETHICAL DILEMMA

Animals of all kinds have been used as medical research subjects for hundreds of years. Although animal research has led to groundbreaking discoveries in vaccines (rabies, whooping cough), treatments (insulin), medicines (penicillin), and surgical techniques (blood transfusions, organ transplants), it remains a controversial subject.

Many people believe experimenting on animals is acceptable as long as the research is intended to improve the quality of human lives and the animals are treated as humanely as possible. Others disagree, believing all life to be equally sacred. They see animal testing as barbaric and unethical, regardless of how humans might benefit.

Fred Banting's idea to use dogs for his insulin research wasn't new. For decades, American and European scientists had been using dogs in pancreatic experiments and studies. But in 1921, animal rights activism was a growing movement, and there was some controversy about how the Toronto insulin pioneers obtained the dogs used for their research. Were they purchased from animal shelters? Or rounded up directly from the streets?

Fred, having grown up on a farm, had a deep respect for nature and a fondness for animals. In his unpublished memoir, he wrote at length about his love of dogs and his conflicted emotions when his subjects died as a result of the lab work. His background also helped to inform his scientific theories. For example, his knowledge of farming techniques led to his sourcing out cow pancreases from slaughterhouses. This discovery allowed Fred and Charley to spare the lives of future lab dogs, and also ushered in a new era in insulin development.

Currently, there are approximately 43 million people around the world who are dependent on insulin for survival. It's probably safe to estimate that insulin has saved well over 100 million lives since its discovery in 1921. But for some, whether medical advancements can ever justify the suffering of animals will always be up for debate.

SOURCES

This graphic novel is based in part on true events. The following resources were consulted in my research:

Banting House National Historic Site of Canada. London, ON.

Bliss, Michael. *The Discovery of Insulin.* Toronto, ON: University of Toronto Press, 2000.

Cooper, Thea and Arthur Ainsberg. *Breakthrough: Banting, Best, and the Race to Save Millions of Diabetics.* Toronto, ON: Viking Canada, 2010.

Fred: Fondation Ressources pour les Enfants Diabétiques (Diabetic Children Foundation). "What Is Type 1 Diabetes?" Type 1 Diabetes. Accessed July 2019. Online.

Insulin Collections. The Discovery and Early Development of Insulin. University of Toronto Libraries, Toronto, ON. Online.

International Diabetes Federation. *IDF Diabetes Atlas,* 9th ed. Brussels, Belgium: International Diabetes Federation, 2019. Accessed August 2019. Online.

International Diabetes Federation. "What Is Diabetes?" About Diabetes. Accessed August 2019. Online.

Klingle, Matthew. "The Multiple Lives of Marjorie: The Dogs of Toronto and the Co-Discovery of Insulin." *Environmental History*, vol. 23, no. 2, April 2018, pp. 368–82.

Mayo Clinic. "Symptoms & Causes." Type 1 Diabetes. Accessed July 2019. Online.

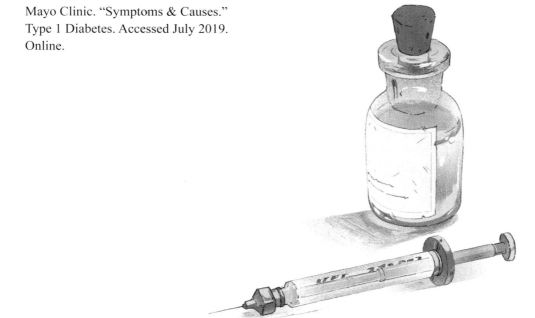

ACKNOWLEDGMENTS

I'm so very grateful to the incredible team at Owlkids for embracing this story with such enthusiasm and bringing this book into the world. With special thanks to my wonderful editors — Karen Li, for her boundless wisdom, guidance, and encouragement; and Stacey Roderick, for her help and support bringing this story across the finish line. A huge thank you to Grant Maltman, curator of the Banting House museum in London, Ontario, for so generously sharing his wealth of knowledge. Hugs to my first readers: Helaine Becker, Suzanne Del Rizzo, Dr. Debbie Donsky, Mahtab Narsimhan, Gordon Pape, Simone Spiegel, and Frieda Wishinsky. Love to my husband, Jordan, and our children, Jonah and Dahlia—each of them living legacies of Fred and Marjorie's work. This story was written in loving memory of my father-in-law, Dr. Gordon Kerbel.

Text © 2021 Deborah Kerbel
Illustrations © 2021 Angela Poon

Owlkids Books acknowledges the financial support of the Canada Council for the Arts, the Ontario Arts Council, the Government of Canada through the Canada Book Fund (CBF) and the Government of Ontario through the Ontario Creates Book Initiative for our publishing activities.

Published in Canada by
Owlkids Books Inc.
1 Eglinton Avenue East
Toronto, ON M4P 3A1

Published in the United States by
Owlkids Books Inc.
1700 Fourth Street
Berkeley, CA 94710

Library and Archives Canada Cataloguing in Publication

Title: Fred & Marjorie : a doctor, a dog, and the discovery of insulin / Deborah Kerbel ; illustrated by Angela Poon.
Other titles: Fred and Marjorie
Names: Kerbel, Deborah, author. | Poon, Angela, illustrator.
Description: Includes bibliographical references.
Identifiers: Canadiana 20200399209 | ISBN 9781771474115 (hardcover)
Subjects: LCSH: Banting, F. G. (Frederick Grant), 1891-1941—Comic books, strips, etc. | LCSH: Banting, F. G. (Frederick Grant), 1891-1941—Juvenile literature. | LCSH: Physicians—Ontario—Biography—Comic books, strips, etc. | LCSH: Physicians—Ontario—Biography—Juvenile literature. | LCSH: Diabetes—History—Comic books, strips, etc. | LCSH: Diabetes—History—Juvenile literature. | LCSH: Insulin—History—Comic books, strips, etc. | LCSH: Insulin—History—Juvenile literature. | LCGFT: Biographical comics. | LCGFT: Nonfiction comics.
Classification: LCC R464.B3 K47 2021 | DDC j616.4/620092—dc23

Library of Congress Control Number: 2020951494

Edited by Karen Li and Stacey Roderick
Designed by Claudia Dávila
Photo credits: pages 52 and 53, courtesy of Thomas Fisher Rare Book Library, University of Toronto

Manufactured in Guangdong Province, Dongguan City, China, in July 2022,
by Toppan Leefung Packaging & Printing (Dongguan) Co., Ltd.   Job #BAYDC90/R1

B   C   D   E   F   G

MIX
Paper from responsible sources
FSC® C104723

ONTARIO ARTS COUNCIL
CONSEIL DES ARTS DE L'ONTARIO
an Ontario government agency
un organisme du gouvernement de l'Ontario

Canada Council for the Arts
Conseil des Arts du Canada

Canadä

Publisher of Chirp, Chickadee and OWL
www.owlkidsbooks.com   Owlkids Books is a division of   bayard canada